Climbing:
From First-Timer
to Gym Climber

Climbing: From First-Timer to Gym Climber

Nate Fitch and Ron Funderburke

FALCON GUIDES

GUILFORD, CONNECTICUT
HELENA, MONTANA

FALCONGUIDES®

An imprint of The Rowman & Littlefield Publishing Group, Inc.
4501 Forbes Blvd., Ste. 200
Lanham, MD 20706
www.rowman.com
Falcon and FalconGuides are registered trademarks and Make
Adventure Your Story is a trademark of The Rowman & Littlefield
Publishing Group, Inc.

Distributed by NATIONAL BOOK NETWORK

British Library Cataloguing in Publication Information available

Library of Congress Cataloging-in-Publication Data available

ISBN 978-1-4930-2764-4 (paperback)
ISBN 978-1-4930-2765-1 (e-book)

∞™ The paper used in this publication meets the minimum
requirements of American National Standard for Information
Sciences—Permanence of Paper for Printed Library Materials,
ANSI/NISO Z39.48-1992.

Printed in the United States of America

Warning: Climbing is a dangerous sport. You can be seriously injured or die. Read the following before you use this book.

This is an instruction book about rock climbing, a sport that is inherently dangerous. **Do not depend solely on information from this book for your personal safety. Your climbing safety depends on your own judgment based on competent instruction, experience, and a realistic assessment of your climbing ability.**

The training advice given in this book is based on the authors' opinions. Consult your physician before engaging in any part of the training program described by the authors.

There are no warranties, either expressed or implied, that this instruction book contains accurate and reliable information. There are no warranties as to fitness for a particular purpose or that this book is merchantable. Your use of this book indicates your assumption of the risk of death or serious injury as a result of climbing's risks and is an acknowledgment of your own sole responsibility for your safety in climbing or in training for climbing.

Rowman & Littlefield and the authors assume no liability for accidents happening to, or injuries sustained by, readers who engage in the activities described in this book.

Contents

Introduction .... *viii*

Chapter One: Welcome to the Climbing Community *1*

Chapter Two: Welcome to the Gym *14*

Chapter Three: Equipment for the Gym *31*

Chapter Four: Instruction *47*

Chapter Five: Climbing Movement *55*

Chapter Six: Bouldering *63*

Chapter Seven: Toproping *70*

Chapter Eight: Lead Climbing *91*

Conclusion *131*

About the Authors *134*

Introduction

In almost every American city and town, there are already lots of ways to stay physically active. There are fitness centers, local sports leagues, country clubs, even personalized exercise regimens, and they all provide a way to enjoy exercise and activity. You don't have to rock climb to be physically active. Similarly, there are already social hubs in every corner of the world: bars and restaurants, clubs and civic organizations, churches and religious groups all bring people together to celebrate, commiserate, or collaborate. You don't have to rock climb to be a part of something bigger than yourself. Lastly, even in the biggest cities, people have dozens of opportunities to step out from their low ceilings and cubicles, to escape confined and cloistered spaces. There are already places where you can let your eyes and awareness take in lofty spaces, and you don't have to rock climb to find them.

All of that is true, and yet we're writing this book to convince you that you should try rock climbing. Among so many options, what does the climbing gym have to offer that a person might not find otherwise? Before we start explaining how to get involved in the sport, it seems like we should convince you that you should even bother in the first place.

We might go ahead and admit that the superiority of rock climbing as a personal and recreational pursuit has been, up to this point, self-appointed. The non-climber looking at climbing culture, norms, and achievements would understandably declare every climber to be self-obsessed, self-aggrandizing, and maybe even delusional. That might be true, but climbers don't spend that much more time congratulating themselves than the admirers of any other sport, social enclave, or club. Every pastime in the country has an association, a club, an organized group of enthusiasts, and a profitable industry propped up around it, and they are probably all ready and willing to have a reader pursue their particular brand of activity. Let us therefore declare that there are quantifiable reasons for eschewing other sports, other social hubs, and embracing a unique escape from the urban humdrum existence.

When we try to convince others that climbing is special and the way we spend our time is superior to all the available options, we do have a distinct advantage over golfers and cross-fit nuts and basketball players and every other person who is so dedicated to their activity of choice: We are right, and everyone else is wrong. George Mallory's circumspect response to the question "Why do you climb?" is often cited by those who wish to understand a climber's motives. We might suggest that it is time for an answer more definitive than "because it is there." Why do we climb? And by extension, why should you?

You should rock climb instead of doing other things because:

- As a physical activity, climbing eventually converts the human form into a trim, angular, and powerful specimen. That makes it a moral good, if you think about it. It's better for an individual, and the species in general, to be fit, flexible, and durable. Plus, you can't condition the musculature into some grotesque proportion through climbing, because climbing perfects the human form.

Whether renaissance painters realized it or not, they were painting climbers.

- As a social activity, climbing eventually reforms and refines the psyche. The recalcitrant become genteel. The reclusive become gregarious. The bombastic become understated. The irritable become sanguine. You name it, climbing is a salve for the human condition. It will sober a drunkard, make a believer of a cynic, impassion the dispassionate. Not to mention how it dissolves solipsism. So, climbers are better spouses, parents, friends, and coworkers.

- As an escape from an otherwise prosaic world, climbing occupies climbing spaces. Whether it's a climbing gym or El Capitan, the arena of climbing is aspirational; it lifts the eyes of its practitioners to the stars and the clouds and the heavens. It's been noted that modernism was a natural response to the heavy weight of industrialism and global wars, the masses dragging their sodden soot-covered brows from their jobs to their graves. But it was actually climbing that saved modernity, not modernism, in case you were wondering. In the dark ages, we built steeples and cathedrals. In the modern age, we build climbing walls.

So, there shouldn't be any lingering mystery that every person should climb. Let us spend the rest of this book explaining how to get started.

CHAPTER 1

Welcome to the Climbing Community

S ince you've decided to join the climbing tribe, there is a lot to learn. We'd like every reader of this text to use its content to expedite the often clunky and mysterious trial-and-error process that often characterizes entrance to any subculture. A quick Google search for "climbing walls" in any area of the country might eventually provide a list of addresses and websites, but that long list of links isn't always that helpful without some frame of reference. Let's get a good idea of what the landscape looks like.

Indoors vs. Outdoors

Climbing in the United States has a long and entertaining history. When you're getting started none of that is really important just yet; you can learn the lore as you go. The first thing you really need to understand is that climbing began as an outdoor pursuit, and many climbers will try to convince you that climbing outdoors is still the purest and most aesthetic aspect of the sport. When you are better inaugurated, you can weigh in on the debate too, but for now don't be distracted by extremists. Climbing started outdoors, but by the middle of the 1990s commercial indoor climbing gyms started popping up all over the country, and their arrival diversified the landscape of American climbing. Today, there are climbing gyms and climbing walls all over the country; in every major city there is at least one, and many cities have as many twelve indoor climbing facilities. Furthermore, most American climbers climb both indoors and outdoors, and we hope you will eventually do both as well. To get started, you need to decide where to start.

We think you should start climbing somewhere that gives you access to the following resources:

- Variety of Terrain. You need lots of different options to learn all the different ways that climbers climb. You'll need a range of available difficulties so you can make a logical progression from easy climbing to challenging climbing. You'll need enough variety to keep things exciting and new.

- Access to Professional Instructors. You'll need to be able to take classes from professional climbing instructors. Some things you can learn on your own, some things you can learn from friends, but a professional teacher is trained to deliver information and skills to you succinctly, accurately, and efficiently. An era ago, climbers had to figure everything out on their own. The pioneering and innovation era of the sport is mostly over for beginners. Professional Instructors take you right to what you want to know, and there is value in that.

- Access to Equipment. Climbing will utilize odd and specific arrays of equipment that are not commonly available at average retailers. You'll need to be able to experiment with new styles, brands, and fittings of specialized equipment that cannot be approximated in a general department store. Furthermore, you'll need some expert guidance when you start making purchases. Climbing equipment can be costly, and informed purchases can save time, money, and heartache.

- Access to Climbing Community. There are a lot of new social norms to learn when you start climbing. You will want to meet everyone. So you need to go somewhere you can meet other first-timers, and second-timers, and beginners, and intermediate climbers, and experts, and professional athletes, and kids, and couples, and singles, and teachers, and armchair quarterbacks, and has-beens, and purists, and generalists . . . everyone in the community. They're all fascinating, and you'll need to figure out where you fit in.

When we survey the landscape of American climbing, we have a hard time finding a place that fits those criteria better than a modern climbing gym. Granted, some cliffs on a given weekend might fit the bill, but it's hard to guarantee that the weather will be

Outdoor Opportunities	Variety of Terrain	Professional Instructors	Access to Equipment	Access to Climbing Community
AAC Craggin' Classic Events	Yes	Yes	Yes	Yes
Red Rock Rendezvous	Yes	Yes	Yes	Yes
Outdoor Climbing Competitions	Yes	No	Maybe	Yes
Local Gatherings	Yes	No	No	Yes

Climbing festivals and gatherings can be a legitimate way to meet the climbing community, but this happens in the gym almost every night.

good on the day you want to get started. By comparison, an indoor climbing facility is likely to provide a first-timer access to those resources on any business day.

Once you've decided to head indoors to get started, it's important to discern the varieties of climbing walls that are available. Indoor climbing walls have become ubiquitous features in multi-use recreation facilities and at large universities, and commercial climbing facilities come in a wide variety of shapes and sizes.

Municipal Climbing Structures

Many city and county recreation departments have added indoor climbing features to their multi-use facilities. It is not uncommon for a racquetball court to be repurposed as a climbing facility. Similarly, basketball teams are becoming accustomed to seeing towering climbing structures as the backdrops of their backboards and baskets. YMCA facilities often include a climbing wall for members. These days, it is not uncommon for public parks to construct bouldering areas that may be enjoyed by any public user any time of day.

These facilities will offer a first-timer a chance to experience climbing. They may even go so far as to teach basic skills like tying in, bouldering and spotting, and belaying. But in general, these multi-use facilities do not provide access to a thriving climbing community, and the instruction and mentorship is usually limited. It is rare to find a municipal program that has a wide and thorough selection of rental equipment, so it's hard to learn what kind of harness and shoes to eventually buy.

In short, municipal climbing structures offer a great chance to physically climb for the first time. But once the climber's appetite for skills and knowledge begins to strengthen, the offerings at these venues quickly seem limiting.

Some smaller climbing walls are great additions to larger recreation facilities, but the offerings in these facilities are usually limited.

University Climbing Walls

Perhaps one step up from their municipal counter-parts, university climbing walls might offer a more inspiring facility, a more impressive array of rental equipment, and staff that are more knowledgeable and better trained. Between students and staff recreating

University climbing walls captivate students, and since there are rarely subsidiary costs for students, faculty, and staff, these facilities are in high demand. If you're not affiliated with the university, you may want call ahead.

As an avid climber, I often find myself in small towns where there is a university climbing wall, but not a commercial or municipal facility. So I've learned to politely poach a student. I wait outside the facility, careful not to make eye contact with security or staff, and when a friendly student comes walking along, I ask to be his/her guest for the day. Students, faculty, and staff are allowed to bring guests to university rec facilities, so I just need someone to get me in the door. I find out the guest fee, I have the exact amount of cash on hand, and I am willing to ply my new friend with belays or beers if necessary.—RF

on the wall, there may even be a thriving community of climbers, faithfully devoted to the climbing wall. These facilities will offer a first-timer a great opportunity to climb for the first time, to learn to belay, experiment with equipment selection and sizing, and learn to lead.

Yet university walls are usually limited to students, faculty, and staff. As a result, the general public may be able to finagle access on a limited basis, or get a good introduction to the sport, but eventually a dedicated and enthusiastic novice will find the hours, the frequent closures, the availability, and the scope of a university wall to be restrictive.

Commercial Climbing Walls

A modern commercial climbing wall is usually part of a towering and impressive facility. It will likely have sectors that are dedicated entirely to lead climbing,

Gym's Attributes	Pros	Cons
Total Climbing Surface Area: The total surface area that is available to climb on. Big Gyms: 20,000–40,000 square feet Medium Gyms: 10,000–20,000 square feet Small Gyms: 1,000–10,000 square feet	Big gyms usually offer lots of options. They are sprawling and impressive structures.	If huge portions of the climbable surface is dedicated to high-level climbers, it might not be great for first-timers.

Gym's Attributes	Pros	Cons
Capacity to Anchor Ratio (CAR): The ratio of anchors to total capacity helps consumers predict how likely they will be to wait in line for a climb when the facility is really busy. It's the maximum legal capacity of the facility divided by the total number of anchors. A big quotient will be more likely to mean longer lines.	The CAR is a cool tool for guessing how crowded a gym might get. If you hope to get on a rope at a popular time of day, the CAR might help you decide where to go.	The CAR can be misleading. Multi-use gyms will have a huge CAR, but maybe the climbing wall is not that popular. Similarly, a lot of the people in a gym with a big CAR might be hanging out in the espresso bar.

Gym's Attributes	Pros	Cons
Professional Instructors	A great gym will have professionally trained and credentialed employees. At a minimum, staff who instruct and supervise climbing should be certified by the Climbing Wall Association. Even better, training from the American Mountain Guides Association ensures a high level of competence and knowledge from the staff.	Professional instructors usually teach and enforce a high standard. So, if you're looking for an environment where the staff will let you do whatever you want (even if it's arguably dangerous), unskilled supervisors usually don't have the expertise to enforce high standards or prioritize safety.
Amenities and Extras	Most modern gyms have a full locker room, retail outlets, concessions, and fitness equipment. Above and beyond that, look for member classes and programming, child care, and affiliations with organizations like the Access Fund or the American Alpine Club.	All these extras add value to the climbing experience, but they also add overhead to the cost of a day pass. Keep that in mind if a budget facility will suffice.

Gym's Attributes	Pros	Cons
Layout and Compartments	A well-designed facility finds ways to segregate different users so different users avoid negatively impacting each other. Classroom climbs, bouldering, and birthday party areas, in particular, don't integrate easily into general use. It's nice when space has been dedicated to these unique activities.	Any facility that attempts to be everything for every climber can't specialize in serving a particular group of climbers. As a result, it's smart to accept a generalized community when you are in a multipurpose facility, or pick a specialized facility.
Height	The height of a climbing gym usually correlates to its size. But some gyms have sprawling floor spaces with relatively short walls. A climb that is 40 to 50 feet tall usually provides ten to twelve body lengths of movement, and that is a very satisfying amount of climbing. Shorter walls can still be fun, but they tend to add difficulty to individual moves since the wall is not tall enough to challenge climbers' overall stamina. At a certain height, bouldering and roped climbing seem too similar to be distinct activities.	Tall walls require a uniquely tall building, so the facility is often located in an industrial center, which is less accessible to urban climbers. Or the facility is built specifically for the wall in an urban area. Those builds are expensive, and the costs usually appear in the price of a day pass or a membership.

Small- and medium-sized commercial gyms are often just big enough to serve the smaller towns and boroughs where they are located.

toproping, bouldering, fitness and exercise, even yoga. It is not uncommon for these facilities to have social and common areas designed solely to facilitate

Larger cities boast large and capacious gyms, with huge square footage, tons of member services, and the full gamut of indoor climbing opportunities. Courtesy of Earth Trek

acquaintances and conversation. These facilities not only have bathrooms but fully featured locker rooms. Climbers will usually find a wide range of rental equipment, snacks and concessions, and perhaps even a retail aspect.

In many US cities, there is more than one commercial climbing facility to choose from, and it's not always easy to tell from a website or a brochure which facility is the right fit. It's important to remember that commercial climbing gyms are running a business, and that makes you a consumer. Be informed, be discerning. Spend your dollars and your time wisely.

Welcome to the Gym

No matter what kind of climbing gym you choose, no matter how many options you may or may not have in your region, there are some commonalities to all gyms. All gyms generally offer five activity categories: general fitness and training, bouldering, autobelaying, toproping, and lead climbing. In this chapter, we'll break down all of the options under the assumption that all five are available in most modern climbing facilities, though some indoor gyms may not offer all five options, and the participant may be limited by a gym's offerings.

General Fitness and Training

Nowadays, the climber has the opportunity to train and pursue general fitness just like any other specialized athlete. That means that most climbing facilities offer resources for that kind of activity. A climber can expect to have access to a variety of cross-training opportunities, including ellipticals, stationary bikes, and treadmills. There is almost always an array of strength training apparatuses, including free weights and arrays of weight lifting systems. Also, unique to climbing gyms, there are usually climbing-specific training areas.

While muscle conditioning and cardiovascular fitness can offer a climber great general fitness gains,

General fitness builds a better climber, and targeting strength training and weight loss can make the difference in performance. Look for a facility that has an array of training opportunities to complement the climbing. Courtesy of Earth Trek

the most rapid performance advances tend to come from climbing-specific training tools like hangboards, campus boards, and system boards. It's worth elucidating that the cutting edge of climbing performance involves as many nuanced and specific training tools and techniques as any other sport. For the novice user, these tools will be of limited use, but it probably helps to know what they are, what they are for, and how too much training too early in a climbing career can be deleterious to connective tissues and joints. It's quite easy to make muscles stronger than the tissues that connect them, or vice versa.

Hangboards

Hangboards give climbers a variety of shapes from which to hang their body weight for increasing increments of time and difficulty. The overall goal is to strengthen the hands and fingers to hold holds of various sizes and shapes. It might be fun and educational for a novice to warm up and then visit the hangboard to experiment with all the different shapes and combinations of holds. Within a few minutes, a climber will be able to know for certain which sizes and shapes are more challenging to hold. We'd discourage much more hangboard training than that for novices, though. A novice will need to slowly and carefully build up to a point where hangboard training can target and augment hand and finger strength. A precocious attempt to use a hangboard can result in painful injuries to the hands and fingers.

Hangboards help a climber train hand, finger, and grip strength. Courtesy of Earth Treks

Campus Boards

Campusing means that climbers monkey up consecutive holds or rungs without using their feet. It's particularly strenuous on the upper body, arms, hands, and fingers. When a climber is ready for it, campusing

Campus boards quickly develop contact strength and upper body strength.

conditions the hands, arms, and fingers to not only hold holds (like a hangboard) but to catch holds while using the arms and upper body to pull the climber's entire body weight. High-performance climbs might require this kind of strength, but it will be of little value to a novice. For a first-timer, it might be fun to simply try campusing a few rungs just to appreciate how difficult high-end climbing actually is.

System Boards

Prior to the prevalence and availability of climbing gyms, many climbers built a small climbing wall in their basements and garages. When they did, many discovered that their ingenuity to design climbs was subsumed by their desire to train. So they tended to just cover the wall in holds and then climb all over the wall. That kind of exercise can be used to emphasize the repetitive use of a particular type of hold, it can emphasize endurance (climbing back and forth and up and down for sustained periods of time), or it can give a climber an opportunity to climb the same move repeatedly without resting.

In a climbing facility, system boards offer climbers a bigger and more versatile opportunity to train in the same way that those early climbers innovated

System boards let a climber cycle through multiple grip styles and gain endurance and contact strength in the process.

in their basements. In a big modern facility though, system boards offer well-padded floors, walls that can be adjusted to different degrees of steepness, and a bewildering array of holds that allow the climber to invent dozens of different hold combinations to train endurance, recovery, and muscle memory.

Bouldering

In the United States, both indoors and outdoors, bouldering has emerged as one of the most popular and vibrant aspects of climbing. For the uninitiated, it's a difficult thing to comprehend, and the easiest way to understand the jargon and norms of bouldering involves a short history lesson.

Imagine the earliest boulderers as rock climbers who sought small climbs on the sides of boulders. Because boulders are smaller, the climbers could easily focus on doing harder moves, and with that emphasis, the difficulty of doing a single move became more sought after than the top of a mountain or a cliff. With that emphasis, climbers sought out problems that required minute adjustments of balance, strength, and precision, so climbers were forced to attempt a climb over and over and over again before discovering the fitness, the sequence, and the stamina needed to climb the boulder.

Eventually, the objective difficulty of climbing a boulder was further subdivided as climbers sought individually difficult moves. They might add more difficulty by starting on lower holds, eliminating holds, climbing an alternative aspect of the boulder, and other shenanigans that seemed quite arbitrary to other climbers. If most climbers are obsessed with achieving

Indoor bouldering seems like an abstract approximation of outdoor bouldering, but the two are more similar than it might seem at first.

an objective summit, boulderers prioritize the journey and the process. As a result, boulderers don't even call their climbs "climbs"; a boulderer climbs a boulder problem, or "problem" for short.

Indoor boulders are colorful and challenging. Look how many problems fit within the surface area. The economy of space is hard to duplicate on natural boulders.

Indoor boulder problems have a clear start and a clear finish. Here, they are marked by colored tags and signage; the finish holds are engraved.

In the gym, bouldering is a cherished pastime. The bouldering section of the gym is typically designated for that purpose entirely. Unlike outdoor bouldering, an indoor boulder problem will typically demarcate holds on which the boulder problem begins and holds on which the problem finishes. Also, the floor of the bouldering area is usually well padded and designed to give plunging boulderers a nice smooth place to land.

The padded floors of a modern climbing gym make falls and tumbles from height much more comfortable.

Some gyms even have boulders that are designed to "top out" like an outdoor boulder problem, which often provides much greater excitement as a climber

Topping out is exciting, and it feels similar to outdoor bouldering.

may be asked to climb to the top of a boulder that is 15–18 feet tall.

Autobelays

Autobelays are mechanical belay cables that are mounted at the top of a climbing wall. From a heavy

Autobelays allow a climber to climb up and lower down without a climbing partner, so self-communication and self-double-checks are important.

The connection of an autobelay is double-checked like any other locking carabiner. A quick squeeze confirms it's locked.

Climbing on an autobelay has five steps. It starts with a connection.

Double-check

Climb *Lower*

Reconnect

mounted housing, a cable and fixed locking carabiner extend down the climbing wall, and remain anchored to the bottom of the wall when not in use. A climber uses the carabiner to connect the autobelay to a climbing harness, and as the climber climbs the autobelay system retracts as the climber ascends the wall. When the climber falls, the autobelay system slowly lowers the climber back to the ground, and the cable can be reattached to the base of the wall, ready for the next climber to come along.

Autobelays can provide a lone climber with an opportunity to do repeated climbs, climbing, lowering, and immediately climbing again. Of course, a good spirit of sharing, refraining from monopolizing an autobelay while others are waiting, is always appreciated. The autobelay can provide a fast and relentless workout whereby solitary climbers can enjoy a session all by themselves.

Toproping

Toproping is probably the most common activity to be found at any indoor climbing facility. To be sure, most modern facilities offer fitness, bouldering, autobelaying, lead climbing, and toproping. But when those facilities are averaged out with smaller gyms, municipal gyms, university gyms, etc., toproping is usually the common denominator.

Toproping has a characteristic rope in place to accommodate one climber and one belayer, most of the time. The rope travels from the ground up to an anchor at the top of the climbing wall and back down to the ground again. There are a handful of variations to this general arrangement, but almost all topropes in

This toproping area is not equipped for any purpose other than toproping.

a climbing gym involve a counterweight arrangement between a belayer on one side of the rope, answered by a climber on the opposite side. Any given gym might have several dozen topropes available; smaller gyms might only have two or three.

1-to-1 counterweight

All topropes require an ascending and lowering climber to be counterweighted by a belayer.

Toprope anchors come in various shapes and sizes, but a double-wrapped bar is common throughout the United States.

A typical toprope setup has some key features: ground anchors (usually optional), a rope stack with a closed system, a belayer, a climbing rope, an anchor, and a climber.

Lead Climbing

Lead climbing is one of the most exciting and energetic activities in the climbing gym. It is about as close as indoor climbers get to managing objective hazards in the same way that outdoor climbers do. In lead climbing, the rope is not securing the climber from above. Instead, the climber connects the rope in increments to the climbing wall as he/she progresses up the wall. The belayer pays out slack to the lead climber in the precise increment needed to keep the climber from falling to the ground or colliding with obstacles as he/she falls.

Lead climbing is usually more strenuous, it involves a greater degree of objective hazard, and it also proposes an arrangement of rope, climber, and belayer wherein human body weights can fall through

Lead climbing areas are often dramatic, steep, and offer unique features. In many facilities, lead climbing is the only way to access these features.

the air or get yanked from the ground. The level of objective hazard means that lead climbing areas are usually segregated from other climbing activities, or at the very least lead climbers are given priority over other users when activities commingle. It's important to stay out of the way when a climber is lead climbing or when a belayer is lead belaying.

CHAPTER 3

Equipment for the Gym

The initial perusal of equipment needed for rock climbing can be exhausting. With all the different disciplines of climbing, all the different manufacturers, and all the publications available, the first-time climber is inundated with a pretty consistent message: Buy lots of stuff! The good news is that none of that messaging is entirely true. No one needs everything all at once, and every climber acquires equipment in phases. The goal of this chapter is to explain when to buy what. Begin with some modest acquisitions. Then, as the climbing becomes more interdisciplinary, purchases can be informed by new relationships with climbing partners and a greater familiarity with all the bewildering variety of brands and accessories and gadgets.

We've divided equipment purchases into four phases, and each phase corresponds with a logical skill progression and the equipment needed to complete that progression. The first phase requires about the same equipment that one might need to visit any fitness program: athletic wear, a water bottle, locker-room toiletries, and a pair of sandals. Certain items will also be valuable on any climbing outing to care for a climber's body and limbs. In the second phase, climbers will want to acquire a basic selection of equipment to personalize the rental equipment they had been using up to that point: climbing shoes, chalk bag, harness, belay device (manual braking device, or MBD), and locking carabiner. In the third phase, a climber will begin to specialize in gym climbing activities, and there will naturally be a need for an additional set of climbing shoes, a new belay device (assisted braking device, or ABD), belay glasses, a climbing rope and quickdraws, brushes, and some climbing-specific apparel. Lastly, the indoor climbing scene may eventually lure a climber into outdoor pursuits. At that time, the equipment that is specific to outdoor climbing might become necessary, but it will rarely be needed to climb in the gym.

Phase 1: "Welcome to the Gym" Equipment

The rental equipment provided by the gym is usually more than adequate for the first few climbing gym outings. Using a pair of rental shoes lets a first-timer

Rental shoes are designed to accommodate lots of differently shaped feet. It's a good place to start, but a bad place to stay. Since you won't be the first user of these shoes, consider wearing socks.

discover the way climbing shoes fit, learn a range of sizes that balance comfort and performance, and experiment with socks and climbing shoes. A rental harness will allow a climber to learn to wear a harness on the true waist, above the iliac crest; most pants are no longer worn this way, so proper harness

A rental harness will work for an introduction to climbing, but it's designed to be versatile, not comfortable.

Are you right- or left-handed?

Rental harnesses and the horizontal belay loop

Many rental harnesses have a horizontal connection point, and that point is also the belay loop. Many climbing schools provide this style of harness because the consolidated tie-in and clip-in point simplifies instruction. It's easier for climbing instructors to teach novices if the functionality of the harness has been simplified. However, the consolidated belay loop and tie-in is rarely used by climbers who graduate from novice status. Horizontal belay loops mean that a belay device necessarily has a left- or right-facing orientation, which makes the belayer set up to accommodate his/her left or right-handedness. Also, the horizontal belay loop tends to result in an acute pressure point just above the climber's waist. It's fine to belay and be lowered like this for one's first climbing experiences, but eventually the more comfortable options become particularly tempting.

fit prompts a reconsideration of how something is supposed to feel on the waistline. A harness is supposed to be worn tightly too, and that takes some getting used to. It's good to get these lessons out of the way without buying full-price equipment. Also, the belay devices provided by the gym are likely to be the belay devices used in the belay classes that will teach you how to belay. So it makes sense to use the rental belay device.

The rental equipment will get a climber through the climbing in Phase 1, but athletic

Most climbing facilities have inexpensive belay hardware available for rental. iStock/ sand86

apparel, a pair of sandals, and a water bottle will rarely be available for rent. These items will also be useful to any fitness-oriented person, even if he/she doesn't become obsessed with climbing, so they are a safe investment.

A pair of comfortable athletic pants or shorts that allow for a full range of motion are critical for climbing. Even though many climbers can be seen wearing denim jeans, a pair of wicking fabric pants that has

Running shorts

Be careful with running shorts. Often, these shorts are not long enough to be pulled below the leg loops of the harness. As a result, the leg loops either dig directly into the legs and skin, or they expose more of the thighs than a climber might be comfortable revealing. It's hard to focus on those first climbs when one is constantly struggling to maintain modesty.

some stretch and a relatively flat waistband is worth every penny. Generally, pants provide some protection from abrasion to the knees and shins, and they are a common choice among many climbers.

A non-cotton T-shirt and sports bra (for women) usually works well for the upper body. Keep in mind that the tail of the shirt will need to tuck into the harness at the waistline, so shirts with a high cut will be particularly difficult to work with.

Sandals allow a gym climber to take climbing shoes off while belaying, visiting the restroom, or exploring the facility in any other capacity. Unlike other footwear, sandals can accompany a climber from climb to climb, and they are quick to step into and slip out of prior to belaying or climbing. While many climbers meander around the gym barefooted, some conscientious efforts at sanitation are usually appreciated by everyone, especially to and from the restroom.

Hair ties, headbands, or a small hat can also be advantageous for getting those flowing locks tucked away. They are especially handy while belaying. Errant hair can easily become entangled in a belay system, so it's nice to keep hair bound and bundled until the climbing is over.

Phase 2: Time to Go Shopping . . . Climbing Gear Shopping

After one or two trips to the gym in rental gear, the padded comfort of a modern climbing harness, the unique contours of a personal climbing shoe, a belay device of choice, some chalk, and a personal care kit will be important acquisitions. Don't rush these purchases, though. Wasting money on equipment simply because it's available will force climbers to adjust their learning to imperfect tools, rather than selecting tools that enable their learning. Often a small local climbing shop will not have a compelling selection of equipment, and if the equipment available isn't just right, then don't be tempted to compromise. At this point, you should know what you are looking for, so don't let an anxious retailer clear out some dusty inventory on you.

Select a harness that fits. It's not as easy as it sounds. Rental harnesses usually come in a one-size-fits-all style, but a personal harness will typically be categorized as XS, S, M, L, or XL, and those sizes will correspond to the circumference of the true waist. Typical women's pant sizes (4, 6, 8, 10, and 12) won't be as useful for purchasing a personal climbing harness as the measurement of the waistline. It's also smart to try the harness on. A size small harness, for example, might be sized for a waistline of 28 to 30 inches. A

Select a harness that meets or exceeds the UIAA standards for climbing harness manufacture.

size medium might be sized for 30 to 33 inches. So a person with a 30-inch waist has an interesting choice to make: to wear a harness at the open-end of small or the closed-end of medium. The size of the leg loops might help make the choice; maybe one set of leg loops fits better. The length of the tails after closing the buckle might make the difference; maybe one sizing leaves too little or too much tail to tuck away neatly. Lastly, the orientation of the gear loops might make the difference; since the belay loop will always be worn in the middle of the body, beneath the navel, the right size harness will position the gear loops evenly on the right and left sides.

Barely enough tail

gear loops are asymmetrical

Find some climbing shoes. An all-around pair of climbing shoes are usually the right choice for a climber in this phase. It's rare that a climber will be ready for an aggressively downturned shoe. Instead, a flat-lasted, all-around shoe that can be worn comfortably for an extended climbing or bouldering session is the ticket. For some reason, retailers will insist on squeezing climbers into uncomfortable shoes. But uncomfortable feet don't perform well. High-performing climbers have learned to wear shoes that a novice would grimace to step into, so don't try to cheat the adaptation process. A beginner should use a beginner shoe for beginner terrain, and incrementally the more aggressive shoes will become both appropriate and comfortable for a foot that has adapted its strength and flexibility for climbing steep walls.

One's first belay device and locking carabiner will probably be one of the most durable and long-lasting equipment choices. Belay hardware will be more likely

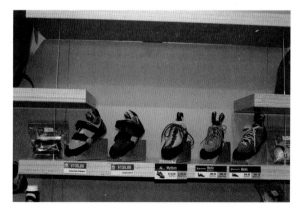

A flat-lasted comfortable climbing shoe is just right for beginners or any climbing that is not severely overhanging. They're also more comfortable.

to survive and sustain the next two phases of a climber's development, so make this choice wisely. Often, it might make sense to select a manual braking device that has an autoblocking function. The autoblock function will never be very useful in a climbing gym, but this piece of equipment will last a long time. So it might be smart to acquire a device with that level of functionality in case those functions are one day needed in other climbing pursuits.

At this point, chalk becomes a persuasive tool as well. In a frenetic gym climbing session, the hands and fingertips can easily become sweaty and clammy. Climber's chalk helps keep that moisture from distracting a climber. The actual "slipperiness" of a climbing hold is hard to estimate, with or without climbing chalk. But most chalk users will attest that a quantified friction coefficient is perfectly irrelevant if a hold "feels" slippery. The dry crisp secure feeling of a chalked grip is hard to forget, and it's even

The carabiner/chalk bag combination won't allow the chalk bag to swivel. Plus, it hangs too low for most people to reach easily.

Carrying a chalk bag on a light belt or cord allows the chalk bag to swivel, and the chalk is in position in the small of the back—easy to reach for almost anyone.

harder to ignore when it's unavailable. So climbing chalk can make a difference. A chalk bag is one of the many choices where an individual climber gets to make an individualized gesture. Chalk bags can be colorful, humorous, eccentric, modest, accessorized, or discreet. Pick one that says something special about you.

Climbing day after day is tough on a body, it's tough on skin, and it can lead to a lot of needless suffering. A personal care kit is a way to stem that tide and get in front of distracting aches and pains. Some cloth athletic tape is helpful for supporting soft tissues and joints. It's also a much tougher bandage than a Band-Aid or adhesive strip. An open cut can be tightly bound with cloth tape so a climber can continue climbing. A few ibuprofen can be nice when muscles and joints are sore. Use of climbing or hand salve after every session can spare cuticles, and help avoid dry skin and calluses. Lastly, fingernail clippers

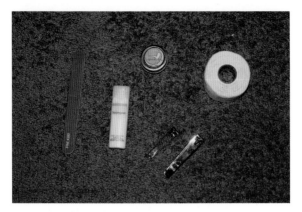

Cloth tape, some finger and toenail clippers, moisturizer, and salve. This personal care kit will keep a climber on track.

and a nail file can keep fingers and nails trim and neat if nails or cuticles tear or break.

Phase 3: Upgrades

By the time climbers have spent some time climbing in a gym, sixty or seventy visits over 6–8 months maybe, a few things will probably start to be true. First, the difficulty at which they can climb will likely have increased. Second, toproping skills will probably start to stir up an interest in lead climbing and lead belaying skills. Lead climbing will likely uncover a need for a new belay device, some lead climbing hardware, and a lead climbing rope. Also, at this point, some new climbing apparel and accessories, designed specifically for climbing by a climbing manufacturer, will start to yield small benefits in performance.

At this point, a climber will likely be able to do the kinds of moves that necessitate a more aggressive climbing shoe, but the most aggressive shoes on the market are not likely to be useful. A slightly down-turned shoe with a well-cupped heel will allow a climber to pull with the heel without having the heel slip out of the shoe, allowing the climber to distribute body weight to smaller footholds, even on an over-hang, and it will begin to prepare the climber's foot for difficulties to come.

These more aggressive models of climbing shoes will be appropriate when climbers' feet are ready for their ambitions.

A climber that has become adept with the use of a manual braking device should be able to add an assisted braking device into the repertoire. Many climbers reverse this logic, because an assisted braking device "assists" and a novice is likely to appreciate that assistance more than an experienced belayer. That might be an appropriate logic for some, but a manual braking device demands precise and fundamentally sound belaying. It won't work otherwise. An assisted

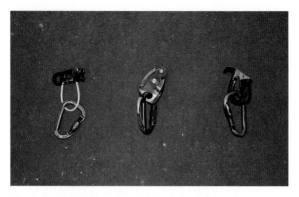

From left to right: a manual braking device, a mechanical assisted braking device, and a passive assisted braking device

braking device, by comparison, will amplify the security of a good belay, but it will also obscure the insecurity of a poor belay. According to that logic, it's better to be a good belayer before learning to use an assisted braking device.

Although most climbing gyms will not require lead climbers to supply their own lead climbing ropes or lead hardware, there are many gyms that do. So it is conceivable, at this phase, that a climber will need to purchase a rope and some quickdraws. In both cases, the equipment should be UIAA endorsed, and in both cases the durability of the equipment is a higher priority than the performance. (The UIAA is [in French] the Union Internationale des Associations Alpinisme, also known as the International Climbing and Mountaineering Federation.) The lead climbing rope should be long enough to get a climber up and down the longest climb in the gym. In almost every facility in the United States, a 60-meter rope is more than adequate. In most facilities, a 60-meter rope can be cut in half, providing two climbing ropes. Twelve quickdraws are usually enough to clip every bolt in the gym, from the floor to the anchors. Again, a durable quickdraw, with a nylon sling and carabiners with a large

Most gyms have all the quickdraws already attached to the wall. If they don't, you'll need your own.

Most gyms provide lead climbing ropes to the consumer. Once again, if they don't, you'll need to provide your own.

clearance, will both endure and enable someone who is learning to clip a rope on lead for the first time.

Phase 4: The Temptation of Outdoor Climbing Equipment

So much of the equipment that adorns the shelves of a climbing shop is designed and intended for outdoor climbing. Indoors, that same array of equipment doesn't look impressive; it looks out of place. So don't be tempted to purchase it, and don't be tempted to bring it to the gym.

The gym can be a great place to meet new friends and mentors, to take clinics, and to learn of the great opportunities that await in other disciplines of climbing. But the need for more equipment will hinge on those opportunities.

CHAPTER 4

Instruction

The climbing gym is an ideal place to start one's climbing career off with sound fundamental skills, a foundation of understanding to build on, and the most accurate and current information available on climbing tools, techniques, culture, and history. One of the best ways to make that start is to hire a climbing instructor or take a class. It might also be possible to meet a mentor, but this strategy can be rife with complications and disappointments. It's important to be thoughtful when selecting the best option.

In this chapter, we'll lay out the pros and cons for each strategy, and we'll take some time to tell a few success stories about each approach. Climbers also need to consider the resources available at each gym and in the local climbing community, scheduling issues, and financial constraints.

Hire an Instructor

Hiring a personal climbing instructor might seem like the kind of thing only celebrities and politicians would do. But from a practical and economic point of view, there can be enormous value. The attention of a one-on-one instructor concentrates the learning experience, and that adds value. A student can learn more in less time, and there is time to indulge lots of tangents, questions, and any need for remedial lessons. A private instructor can quickly adapt to the way an individual needs to learn. Professional climbing instructors are trained to address multiple learning styles when they teach a group, because it is difficult to anticipate or predict the combination of learning styles in a given group of randomly assorted students. So lessons take time as the instructor strives to facilitate careful explanations (for theoretical or language-oriented learners), demonstrations (for visual learners), and hands-on practice (for kinesthetic learners).

In a one-on-one lesson, the instructor can quickly gain an insight into the learner's unique style and tailor all lessons individually. It's a powerful and valuable resource. But every person out there selling climbing instruction might not necessarily have the skill, professionalism, or willingness to be a good educator. So, the individual that elects to hire a private instructor should be an informed consumer.

Climbing instructors are credentialed by three organizations in the United States, and they tend to seek those credentials for different reasons. As a consumer, it is advisable to match up the instructor's credentials with your goals.

American Mountain Guides Association (AMGA)–Certified Climbing Wall Instructor (CWI)

AMGA CWIs have the most training and the most esteemed certifications in the climbing wall industry. They are trained to high technical standards, and, more importantly, they are trained to be good educators. Their coursework and assessment as teachers requires an amassed résumé of prerequisite experience, and they spend more than 21 hours being scrutinized

An AMGA-certified climbing wall instructor has one of the most rigorous credentials that climbing wall employees can attain in the United States.

by their examiners before attaining certification. However, the AMGA CWI course is expensive, and the long list of prerequisites are prohibitive for many climbing instructors. There might not be an AMGA-certified CWI working in your area, or a CWI might not work for the facility you choose to attend.

USA Climbing Certified Coach

The best coaches of climbing teams and professional climbing athletes in the United States are trained and certified by USA Climbing. The emphasis of their credential is slightly different than their counterparts in the industry. They are athletic coaches, and their expertise moves more toward enhancing and augmenting performance, designing training routines, and preventing injury. If your facility fields competitive youth or adult teams, odds are they have professional instructors available as USA Climbing coaches.

Climbing Wall Association (CWA) Climbing Wall Instructors

The CWA CWI is trained to be a fluent climbing gym employee, and they have achieved a minimum standard in technical and instructional proficiency. Many climbing wall employees are CWA-certified CWIs. The biggest difference between these instructors and their peers is a simple matter of experience and training. CWA CWIs are not required to have the same amount of prerequisite experience, necessarily, and their training and examination process is less rigorous. They are trained to be skilled climbing wall employees, but not necessarily skilled educators. In classes with a high student-to-instructor ratio, floor supervision, and customer service, they excel, but they might not be prepared to adapt multiday curricula to the progression of an individual learner.

Other Experience and Credentials

Other experience and credentials are always impressive. For example, a degree in education or sports science, experience as an experiential educator, or other certifications from the AMGA or less prestigious training entities might all inform and enhance a climbing instructor's credentials. The tricky question is: Do those other experiences and credentials necessarily pertain to indoor climbing tools, techniques, history, and culture? If they do not, an instructor adorned with extra experience and credentials is merely more interesting, not necessarily more effective.

Take a Class

If an aspiring climber doesn't have the resources available to hire a private instructor, the next best option is to find one of those same instructors working at a higher ratio, teaching a class or clinic. Clinics do not always result in the same efficiency, since each student's learning experience is shared, but it is a way to get access to accurate information and meet other climbers who probably share the same values and experience.

There are a few important questions to ask when shopping for just the right class. First, ask about the maximum student-to-instructor ratio. The student-to-instructor ratio will give you an idea about how much your learning experience is going to be diluted by your fellow students.

Next, ask which classes at which time of day are the most and least popular. More than once, a student

Climbing gyms usually offer an array of educational programming to members and customers.

[Class Shopping Questionnaire]

Be sure to ask about . . .	What you want to hear . . .	What should make you nervous . . .
Student-to-instructor ratio	6:1 allows a student to collaborate and get attention from the instructor.	If the gym allows large ratios, or the max ratio is not fixed, you could end up in a massive class.
What times are the most popular?	You are looking for a less popular time to get that incidental low ratio.	Our classes are never popular. Or our classes are always super crowded.
What is the "classroom" like?	The gym has a separate learning environment, free of distractions.	We teach in the same space that you will be climbing.
Are there any prerequisites?	If you want a beginner class with a beginner experience, you want few if any prerequisites. If you want a more advanced class and experience, you want more prerequisites.	Mismatched content and prerequisites. A beginner class with tons of prerequisites. An intermediate or advanced class with none.

has strategically attended a less popular class time and incidentally enjoyed a one-to-one student-to-instructor ratio.

Also ask about the learning environment. Are classes taught in the same crowded and noisy floor space as the rest of the facility? That might not be an optimal space to learn. Look for a facility advertising an ideal learning environment for you.

Lastly, ask if there are any prerequisites. Prerequisites tell you a lot about the scope of the class, and they also tell you about what your experience is going to be like. If there is a climbing movement class and it has no prerequisites, it tells you that the class is great for a total novice, and maybe that's what you are looking for. If, however, there are a handful of prerequisites, you can be assured that you have found a course that is either part of a series or is designed to instruct an intermediate or advanced student.

Find a Mentor

The traditional learning relationship in climbing happens between a mentor and her mentee. A mentor takes a liking to a young climber, through some coincidental twist of the cosmos, and the mentor guides the mentee through all the experience and expertise she has accrued through years of study and practice.

When that kind of relationship happens, it is special and rewarding, and we wouldn't presume to discourage it. However, many aspects of traditional mentorship in modern climbing are problematic. First, climbing has grown so rapidly that mentees far outnumber mentors. Finding an effective mentor can feel like finding a unicorn.

Second, many climbers are eager to assume the mantle of mentor. After all, it is satisfying, flattering, and self-gratifying in a lot of ways to be someone's mentor. But eagerness does not necessarily qualify someone to be a mentor. It is valuable and prudent to understand a mentor's motives, and as soon as you do, the worthiness of your prospective mentor either shines through or it is cast in relief.

Third, even if a mentor's motives are pure, it is difficult to evaluate the person's credibility, from the perspective of a mentee. No one certifies or credentials an informal mentor. The relationship is informal (not professional), after all. At some point, the mentor's qualifications are taken on faith, and we'd recommend that kind of choice be made judiciously.

CHAPTER 5

Climbing Movement

C limbing is not an intuitive way to move, and humans do not have an evolutionary predisposition to climbing, the way our primate cousins do. In this chapter, we will explore some of the initial hurdles first-timers are likely to encounter on their first climbs, and we will explore a few exercises to shorten the learning curve.

Why Climbing Will Be Challenging at First

There are a few unfortunate and inescapable realities associated with bipedal locomotion. As humans, we've evolved over millennia to stand upright, move upright, and our hands and arms are not used for locomotion. At least, as we move, we do not distribute weight to our forelimbs as quadrupeds do. From an evolutionary point of view, that has liberated our hands to carry tools, carry our offspring, or wipe sweat away from our hairless brows. It also means that our brains are hardwired to initiate steady and precise weight transfers from one foot to the next, without any of our body weight distributed to our hands and arms.

Climbing demands that we do something that our brains have not evolved to do. It demands that we learn to move like a quadruped, distributing weight to all four limbs, as precisely and seamlessly as we have always done with only two. It will take practice.

At first, the brain is likely to overcompensate by overgripping and stubbornly attempting to distribute *all* body weight to the forelimbs. So you're going to feel fatigue, deep burning muscular fatigue in the hands and forearms. Second, when you feel the slightest bit of fear, like the feeling that you might fall for the first time, your natural response will be to tighten into a fetal position, close your eyes, and pull your face into the shelter of your arms or chest, which is the worst place for your eyes to be when you really need to pay attention to your footing, and redistribute your body weight, equitably, to lower limbs.

Nothing we can write in this book can override the challenges first-timers will face on these initial climbs. What we can do is draw attention to the

At first, it's difficult to learn to climb, because the new environment is so scary. We overgrip, we lose focus, and we try to get close to the wall. This is a natural response to fear that climbers unlearn.

challenge and the nature of the challenge so learning and growth can happen.

Weight Shift

On the first climbs, it is important to develop body awareness, to think about and feel all aspects of the body as one climbs. Body awareness can be practiced at any time. It's important to calm the mind, clear away distractions, and consciously feel every part of your body, one step at a time. You start with the feel of skin against clothing. The feel of the skeleton and muscles resting on the heels or buttocks. The sensation of air passing through nostrils, or one's own tongue sitting in the mouth and the saliva around it.

Body awareness is critical because your brain is unlikely to pay attention to what your body is doing unless you condition it to. Without body awareness, a first-timer is likely to focus on superficial sensations like fatigue, temperature, or the texture of the holds. Instead, a climber needs to focus on where body weight is. Is it on the feet or on the arms? If it's on the arms, consciously distribute it to the feet. To help improve body awareness, first-timers can do a series of drills to help them understand some basic principles of climbing movement.

Starfish System Board Drill

One way or another, the hand bone is connected to the foot bone. With a grid of holds, it's is easy to experiment with, and eventually anticipate, how the position of hands and feet relative to one another makes it easier or harder for climbers to distribute weight to their legs and feet.

With both hands on a single hold and the feet at shoulder width, a climber can feel weight distributing to both feet. Practice shifting from left to right.

When climbing vertical walls, it's advantageous and restful to find a triangular body position, where the climber's weight can be distributed to the feet.

With the hands positioned wide and the feet positioned narrowly, the climber's body forms a V position. From this position it's easy to shift weight from one arm to the other, and it's also easy to feel the instability that results from trying to release one hand without adjusting the feet and the center of gravity.

When the feet are to the right or the left and the hands are holding holds on the opposite side of the body, the climber's body forms the backslash position. It's easy to feel how much body weight is on the arms in this position. Be sure to try both sides.

Leaning back on one's arms with higher footing will happen a lot. Climbers learn to roll and reach from the backslash position.

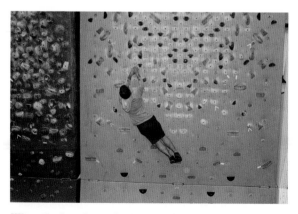

When the hands get farther and farther from the footing, climbers have to tighten the abdominal core to keep their feet on the wall. This elongated backslash is strenuous.

Making a long reach is a complex motor skill. Climbers have to point their toes, tighten the core, make the reach, and then try to control their footwork once they have their desired hold in hand.

Movement

The Starfish drill helps first-timers understand how to be body-aware of their limbs in a series of stationary positions. But that isn't climbing. Climbing is movement: sequencing the limbs from one position to the next to move in any direction. It's a liberating experience because bipeds learn to live and thrive by using a two–dimensional plane, but climbing is three-dimensional, adding depth and verticality to motion.

The Ladder Eliminate

Start with obvious sequential movement, something like a ladder, or simple rows and columns of hand footholds. Make a simple lap up, and count the number of hand- and footholds used. Now, through sequential laps, focus on using fewer and fewer hand- and footholds. Eventually you should be able to cut down the total number of holds by 50 percent. Economy of movement is a major theme in climbing, and it won't come naturally. It will only happen through dedicated practice.

Unlearning Evolutionary Conditioning

Learning to climb can't be done in a single session. It takes time to unlearn a million years of evolutionary conditioning. First-timers should strive to understand the nature of challenges they will face, become body-aware, learn to counter their brain's impulse to squeeze handholds and instead redistribute weight to the lower limbs, resist the urge to crouch and collapse when anxious, learn how the positions of the limbs make it harder and easier to distribute body weight equitably, and strive for economy of movement. These are the first major hurdles.

In time, specialized and nuanced techniques will be needed, but it is important not to get too bogged down in all that. It's also important not to be overwhelmed by too much jargon and vocabulary. For the first time, big holds are attractive. Small holds are difficult to hold. All the jargon associated with those two functional realities are effectively irrelevant. There will be time and opportunity to learn that in the future. For now, focus on the main challenge: Teach your brain and your body to become a quadruped.

CHAPTER 6

Bouldering

One of the first activities that a first-timer will enjoy is bouldering. Many climbers discover such an unencumbered simplicity to bouldering, they never desire to venture into other aspects of climbing. It's easy to understand the attraction. Bouldering involves short enjoyable climbs. It's social and collaborative, and the challenges pile right on top of each other. With enough practice and dedication, so do the successes.

A first-timer will not need to learn tons of new technical information or peculiar rope techniques in bouldering. But that doesn't mean that there is nothing to learn. Since bouldering ultimately means that a climber is climbing without a rope, staying safe *and*

Some boulder problems are really tall. At a certain height, it's important to learn to climb decisively and avoid falling.

having fun can be tricky goals to reconcile. There is a point where bouldering exposes almost every climber to challenging moves high off the ground, and the climber must decide to go for it or retreat. Even

A brief glossary of terms related to climbing movement

Yosemite Decimal System	The Yosemite decimal system, YDS for short, is a numeric system designed to characterize the difficulty of a rock climb. It always starts with a 5, and then the second number numerically classifies the difficulty. The higher the number, the harder the climb. In the upper grades, the climbs are subdivided by a third designation, a letter grade. The letter grade further distinguishes difficulty from a to d. For example, a 5.10a should feel easier than a 5.10d.
Onsight	When climbers ascend a route or problem without any foreknowledge, when they either intuit or guess the moves while on the climb for the first time, they have "onsighted" the climb.
Flash	When climbers have some foreknowledge of a route or boulder problem (they tried parts of it, they watched someone do it, they studied it closely from the ground), but they execute the climb on their first attempt, they've "flashed" the climb.
Project	A climb that cannot be flashed or onsighted requires sustained effort. It's a project that the climber must attempt over and over in order to climb without falling. Climbers "work their project" or they're "projecting" in order to achieve eventual success. Some projects are never achieved.
Redpoint or Send	Eventual success on a project is called a redpoint or a send. "I finally redpointed my project last night. I thought I would never send that thing."

though it feels like an unbridled playground, bouldering areas are taller and more consequential than your neighborhood monkey bars.

As you start to boulder, pay close attention to how problems start and finish. Survey every hold along the course of the problem. The joy and challenge are two-fold. First, you want to be physically challenged by a problem, but you also want to practice reading a problem, anticipating a move before it's ever necessary to physically execute. Bouldering uniquely consolidates the most difficult moves into a discrete sequence over a relatively short distance. So the physicality is acute and enjoyable, but don't let the short length of the difficulties deceive you. Boulder problems are devilishly created, and it takes practice to read a problem and anticipate the bizarre movements that have been designed to perplex and elude even the most perceptive climbers.

Like many pursuits in climbing, your motivations for bouldering may take many forms. Maybe you'll want to boulder in order to become physically stronger, to hone your ability to read and anticipate difficult movement. Maybe you'll just enjoy bouldering as a way to diversify your roped climbing. Maybe you'll use boulder problems to train for specific difficulties or strengthen specific weaknesses. Maybe you'll cherish the social and collaborative aspects of bouldering.

Boulderers self-identify with the discipline of bouldering, and they are content to challenge themselves and push their personal limits within that discipline entirely. To keep this pathway going, it's important to think about the long-term health and care of soft tissues, especially tendons and joints that can be particularly strained by bouldering difficulties. In general, avoiding climbing through minor injuries,

Bouldering Pathways	Session Characteristics	Ideal Problem Selection
Boulderer	You'll want to warm up on two or three problems at each grade all the way up to your project grade. You'll work the project, flash and onsight attempt, for most of your session. Before quitting, you'll warm down on a few problems well beneath your project level.	Warm-up problems. Flash and onsight attempts, open new projects. Remainder of session dedicated to open projects. Warm-down problems.
Trainer	You'll find problems and circuits that mimic difficulties you are having on roped climbs. Your warm-ups and projects will consistently reflect those difficulties, or you will devote yourself to a training scheme that is sympathetic to those difficulties.	Warm up on problems that approximate the YDS grades of your roped warmup. Proceed to training regimen.
Socializer	You'll look for a group of climbers who are gathered around a problem or a section of problems that you have climbed or projected before. You'll join in, encouraging and collaborating with others, unconcerned about the outcome of the session.	Warm up. Find a session with kindred climbers and join in.

Boulderers pursue challenging problems and try to push the boundaries of their abilities on every climb.

getting adequate rest and recovery, and supplementing sessions with thoughtful conditioning can ensure a long and sustainable bouldering pathway.

Rock climbers enjoy and respect bouldering as a training method, and that's why they can often be found in the bouldering area of any gym. But their ambitions are rarely within that realm. A trainer uses bouldering to hone in on a rope project. Boulder problems often simulate the most difficult cruxes of a roped climber, and climbers who spend time bouldering develop proficiency reading a crux before attempting to climb the crux. Similarly, the bursts of power needed to climb a route with multiple cruxes can be simulated by bouldering consecutive problems without significant rest.

Some climbers use bouldering to train for other objectives, like roped climbing. You can often see these folks bouldering in their harnesses, which makes sense if they're training for roped difficulties.

Socializers like bouldering; otherwise they would just join a book club. But their affection for bouldering is inextricable from the scene that often surrounds a boulder problem. Climbers sit together watching each other take turns on a single problem (or group of problems). Each climber's attempt is applauded, and successes result in small jubilations. It's no wonder why the socializer loves bouldering. It's rare to find a sport where individual successes feel so communal. For many, this scene is inspiring and comforting, regardless of the failures or successes that might characterize an individual performance.

CHAPTER 7

Toproping

Roped climbing on an indoor climbing wall can be an engaging and invigorating way to climb. It's also a team endeavor; it's most commonly done in teams of two. The climber climbs; the belayer belays. Belaying is an engaging form of active rest, and it feels good to take responsibility for another climber in this way. The relationship is vital, it's real, and it's intimate. There are not many activities that make two people interrelate in this way, and strong friendships and bonds form quickly.

For the climber, it can be stimulating to do longer stretches of moves than a boulder problem might present. It's a worthy challenge to compound the difficulty of climbing with an intense emotional experience, like being high off the ground. And, we might as well admit it, it feels good to achieve the summit, the pinnacle, the apex, to go until you can go no farther.

To transition from being a first-timer to a seasoned gym climber, it will be important to tie the figure-8 follow-through consistently, efficiently, correctly, and elegantly. It will be important to know how to belay with both a manual and an assisted braking device. Then you will want to toprope with purpose. You'll want to be out there running laps for fun or fitness, training for some objective elsewhere, projecting, or working on your onsight/flash abilities. Lastly, you'll want to understand how to interact gracefully and politely with other parties, and what to do if you find yourself at the gym alone.

Figure-8 Follow-Through

The most common knot in climbing is the figure-8 follow-through. For some climbing organizations, like the AMGA for example, the figure-8 follow-through is part of the iconography of the association (the knot is actually a part of the AMGA logo). It's a strong knot. At high loads, higher than any human body weight could create, it has a predictable failure mechanism, snapping the rope underneath the first biting bend of the knot. That's attractive. Climbers want knots and hitches that behave predictably when tied correctly. Also, when tied correctly, the figure-8 follow-through is secure. It takes two separate gestures of the tail to destabilize the load-bearing properties of the knot. The figure-8 follow-through is quick to tie, and relatively easy to untie after it's loaded. It's also easy to teach and easy to learn, because it's tied in three distinct steps, and each step provides a road map for

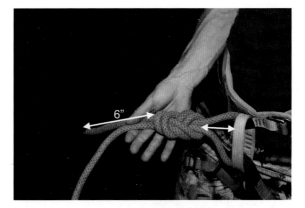

A properly tied figure-8 follow-through is well dressed, positioned right beside the harness, and has a 6-inch tail.

the step that follows. Lastly, when tied correctly, the knot is easy to recognize from a distance, it's easy for the parties in a climbing team to double-check and inspect, and it's easy for all climb teams in proximity to one another to keep an eye on each other.

It's interesting therefore, given the strengths and weaknesses of the knot, and all the reasons climbers gravitated to the knot in the first place, all the reasons that it has become iconic, that so many climbers will tolerate sloppy knots, odd positions of the knot, and odd gestures of the tail.

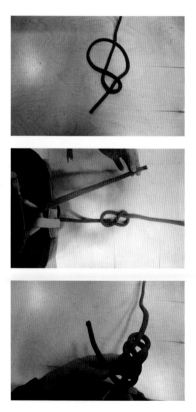

Start with a figure-8 knot.

Pass the tail through the harness's tie-in points.

Retrace, or follow through, the original 8 with the tail.

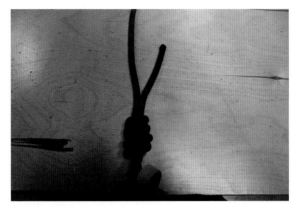

Manipulate the knot to guarantee a 6-inch tail, a small gap between the knot and the harness, and well-dressed symmetry.

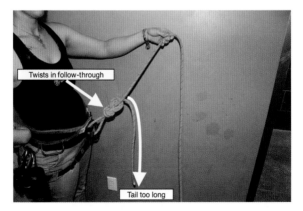

Twists in follow-through

Tail too long

A little attention to detail and practice could clean this knot up. Dress the knot, shorten the tail, and cinch the knot closer to the harness.

The gap between this knot and the harness is so large, it's easy to entangle holds, carabiners, and body parts.

The Kentucky Tucky is a tail finish that was popularized in the Red River Gorge of Kentucky. Aside from a stylistic flourish, it has no practical purpose.

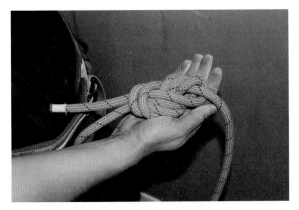

Putting an impressively regal collar on the 8, the Yosemite finish also does little more than adorn an otherwise symmetrical knot.

A barrel knot, popularly misunderstood to be a "safety" knot, simply adds bulk to an already secure and sturdy knot.

Belaying

Once connected to the climbing rope with a properly tied figure-8 follow-through, a climber will anxiously await a belay, and belaying is one of the solemn and exciting duties that climbers must perform. It can be fun, but it's a serious and important job. All belaying requires effective communication, a series of double-checks, and fundamentally sound execution.

Communication has to unambiguously relay action from climber to belayer, and vice versa. First-timers need to learn that most climbers communicate in two different ways. They revert to formal and institutional communication protocols when they are communicating with people they don't know very well, but they also use an agreed-upon familiar system when the climber and belayer get to know each other and communication can be more casual. Usually, in times of duress, or when communication becomes challenging, even the closest friends will revert to those formal and institutional commands.

Communication usually provides a logical time for the climber and belayer to double-check all the critical links in the climbing and belaying system. That's a good idea. It can feel hokey at first, but soon the quick inspection can happen at a glance, in fractions of a second. The critical links are the harness buckles, both ends of the rope, the belay device and carabiner, the figure-8 follow-through, and the anchor. There are also noncritical links that could be addressed if discovered. These things could result in a mishap and demonstrate a team that is undisciplined and imprecise

Climber	Belayer	Corresponding Action
"On Belay, [Name of Belayer]?"		The climber displays his/her tie-in, harness, helmet, and climbing rope while inspecting the belayer's harness, belay setup, helmet, and ground anchor. The belayer checks the climber. When all these double-checks are affirmed, the belayer can confidently continue to communicate.
	"Belay on, [Name of Climber]?"	The belayer begins a vigilant, attentive, and serious administration of the belay system.
"Climbing, [Name of Belayer]."	"Climb on, [Name of Climber]."	The climber begins climbing.
"Tension, [Name of Belayer]."	"I've got you, [Name of Climber]."	The belayer pulls all latent elasticity out of the belay system so the climber can lean back and put weight on the rope. When the rope is tight, the climber leans back and relinquishes all body weight to the rope.

Climber	Belayer	Corresponding Action
"Ready to lower, [Name of Belayer]."	"Lowering, [Name of Climber]."	When the climber is ready to lower, the belayer lowers the climber gently and smoothly to the ground.
"Off Belay, [Name of Belayer]."	"Belay off, [Name of Climber]."	If the climber is safe, firmly footed, and secure, there is no longer a need for belay, and the belay system can be deconstructed.
Conditional Communication		
"Slack, [Name of Belayer]."		The belayer provides one arm length of the slack. If the climber requires slack, he/she will request more.
"Up rope, [Name of Belayer]."		If the climber needs the belayer to move slack out of the belay system, the "up rope" communication is given. In this circumstance the climber should also stop climbing until the slack is removed from the system.

The climber checks the belayer's belay setup, harness buckles, locking carabiner, and readiness to belay.

The belayer checks the climber's tie-in, harness, buckles, and readiness to climb.

when they are overlooked: the orientation of the belay device, the dressing of the figure-8 follow-through, the position and organization of the climbing rope, a parallel and untwisted climbing rope, and the orientation and setup of a ground anchor.

Once the climber and belayer have communicated, and all the double-checks have happened, a toproping climber will slacken the rope system, and the belayer must belay that slack out of the system, mitigating most (if not all) fall consequences. Accomplished belayers understand and accept certain indisputable facts about how their bodies work, how their brains work, and the consequences of a misstep when belaying. First, most humans have remarkably powerful grip strength. Even infant hands and fingers grip tightly, relative to their tiny body mass. But, certain positions of the hand, arm, and fingers can augment grip strength. When the hand is beneath the waistline, or the transverse plane, the neutral grip is the natural resting position of the hand, and it is the position in which the hand has the most grip strength.

Grip strength is slightly diminished when the hand rotates into the pronated grip position, and it is significantly diminished in the supinated grip position, when the hand is beneath the transverse plane.

Next, belayers understand that their attention span is finite, and unpredictable. Any number of things at a climbing gym could produce legitimate distractions. Even in an empty gym, the brain is naturally susceptible to gaps in focus and attentiveness. So a smart belayer tries to belay in a way that is likely to arrest a fall if the climber falls during one of these lapses in attention.

Lastly, a belayer respects that a failure to understand any of these indisputable realities could result in catastrophic mistakes. Belay-related mistakes happen, but they are not because of some divine power, or the

> I am one of the foremost authorities on belaying in the United States, if one can claim such a thing. I have made belay errors. I have made belay errors in the last six months. If I can make belay errors, then no one is immune. I'm just glad that I always stack the odds in my favor, and that means that the errors I made ended up being inconsequential. —RF

whim of the cosmos. They happen because people make mistakes. A belayer accepts that we are all susceptible to mistakes, and that inspires vigilance, reflection, and dedication.

Because of the indisputable facts about the human body, the human brain, and the human condition, three fundamental principles about belaying have stood the test of time. No matter what device belayers use, no matter the context in which they belay, no matter if they are right- or left-handed, the following principles will help to discern effective belaying from ineffective:

1. Always have a brake hand on the brake strand of the rope.

2. At the most vulnerable times, when the hand is sliding on the rope, make sure the rope is in the position of maximum friction.

3. Use the hands and limbs in the positions of their natural strength.

The Guide Hand reaches down and pinches the rope under the brake hand.

The Brake hand slides up the rope.

MBDs and ABDs

Manual braking devices (MBDs) are great tools to learn on because they provide instant feedback to a belayer who is still learning the fundamental principles of belaying. If the rope leaves the braking plane of the device, it's harder to hold. If the hand is in an unnatural position, the rope is harder to hold. It's great for learning. But manual braking devices are highly consequential. There is no backup. If a belayer is holding a climber's body weight, or lowering, with a manual braking device, any mistake from the belayer at this point could be catastrophic for the climber. That's why climbing instructors often serve as backup belayers when belayers are first learning; it's a dangerous situation for students to be in.

We would stipulate that backups are supremely valuable to climbers, because the consequences of

Manual braking devices will not arrest a climber's fall or lower without a vigilant brake hand on the rope. There is no backup. So backup belays like the one pictured above are nice gestures when using a manual braking device.

Manual Braking Devices and Assisted Braking Devices

	Advantages	Disadvantages
Manual Braking Devices	• MBDs help a belayer learn because they give instant feedback if the belay technique is inappropriate. They don't work well unless they are used correctly. • Small and lightweight • Inexpensive • All the varieties function approximately the same way in the gym. Learning one style translates to almost all styles.	• Unless another person gives a backup belay, MBDs do not offer a margin of error when catching falls or lowering. • It is difficult to keep the brake hand stationary while lead belaying, and that results in less overall economy of movement. • Catching lead falls and supporting a lead climber can be strenuous. Many people are not strong enough.
Assisted Braking Devices	• When properly used, ABDs give belayers a backup when catching and lowering. • An assisted braking function makes it less strenuous to support a leader and catch falls. • It is usually possible to keep the brake hand stationary while lead belaying, resulting in overall movement economy.	• ABDs are usually more expensive. • Each ABD model has unique quirks that have to be understood and mastered. Knowing one doesn't mean you will know them all. • The assisted braking function will allow a poor belayer to ingrain bad habits.
Key Lesson:	Because both MBDs and ABDs have advantages and disadvantages, neither tool emerges as a clear stand-alone winner. We recommend first-timers learn with an MBD and the watchful eye of a backup belayer, for both toproping and lead belaying. Once their belay skills are ingrained and trustworthy, they can experiment with an ABD model of their choice and graduate to the more sophisticated device.	

The Petzl Grigri has defined the genre of mechanical assisted braking devices.

The Black Diamond Pilot is compact, lightweight, and easy to use. It's a great tool for the gym climber who seeks a margin of error in his/her belaying.

not having backups are predictably severe. Consider the belay team that selected a manual braking device one night in the gym. They were doing everything carefully and prudently. The climber was climbing; the belayer was belaying effectively with an MBD.

The Mammut SMART and the variety of passive assisted braking devices on the market provide backups to any belayer.

Suddenly, the climber snapped one of the holds off the wall (cracked holds can break easily). The hold fell from 30 feet and struck the belayer right between the eyes. The dazed and reactive belayer dropped the climber.

An ABD probably would have arrested that climber, giving the belayer an effective backup in this rare and scary scenario.

Toprope Climbing

Climbing a toprope is really enjoyable. One quickly adjusts to the fact that a rope rises up from the tie-in, and the climber's head and eyes must find a way to maneuver around the rope. Some climbs, like overhangs, make this particularly challenging. Even that scenario can be learned and adjusted to.

On any toprope, for any set of motives, a climber should strive to move from the bottom of the climb to the top without falling or resting on the rope. The rope is a backup, and when its presence is relied upon entirely, that's not climbing, it's rope hanging punctuated by climbing. Climbers call it hangdogging. It's inelegant, it's slow, and it's not any fun. If a climber

There are lots of topropes hanging, but every rope won't accommodate every climb. Find the rope that is on the fall line for the climb that you want to do.

Surrender to the rope and the belayer. Lean back in the harness and push off the wall with the feet.

finds him/herself hangdogging, it might be time to lower or transition to an easier climb.

Within that simple ethic, much like bouldering, climbers tend to toprope for a lot of different reasons. Some climbers like to get a workout, and so they may climb up and climb down (instead of lowering).

Some climbers are training for a specific goal, like a big outdoor rock climb. So they may attempt to climb consecutive pitches quickly, with little rest in between. Some toprope climbers like to project, and some like to flash/onsight. Toproping is happy to accommodate all those goals and ambitions.

Autobelays

Autobelays come in a few shapes and sizes, but they all function similarly. A cable with a locking carabiner is attached to the climber's belay loop. As the climber climbs, the cable retracts, and when the climber falls or lets go of the wall, the autobelay system smoothly lowers him/her to the ground.

Believe it or not, this vital connection between the climber and the cable, the carabiner, is sometimes overlooked. We'd recommend that the same belay communication and double-checks that precede any climb also precede the use of an autobelay. It might seem a little hokey to talk to yourself this way, but having an accident on an autobelay feels a lot worse.

CHAPTER 8

Lead Climbing

Toproping and bouldering pursuits can provide years and years of satisfactory experiences and progression, but eventually the question of lead climbing will enter a climber's consciousness. Peer pressure can be persuasive. There are social and cultural cues that make lead climbing seem like an inevitable progression. But we think there is a better reason to learn to lead climb. Look at the vast and expansive spaces that constitute the lead climbing sectors of a climbing gym. These are aspirational designs. They soar and arch and rise above the viewer, demand that eyes crane farther and farther back, turning whole revolutions, in order to take in the

This lead climbing sector is imposing and beautiful. A climber has to learn to lead to experience a place like this.

enormity of these spaces. There are no webs of dangling cords and ropes interfering with the uninterrupted space. The only way to dance with that space is to take the rope up there yourself.

Leading is much more than dragging a rope, however, and we can't flirt with those austere spaces by ourselves. Learning to lead also means learning to lead belay, learning to take falls, and learning to manage a new set of risks that toproping and bouldering largely avoid. It might be more accurate to say that lead climbers and their belayers comanage the risks of lead climbing. They become a team, and they take turns enjoying the expansive space above them.

For the first-timer lead climber, there is a lot to learn. We've broken this section of the book into four parts. In the first part, we want aspiring lead climbers to look at their personal motivations and ask some questions that dictate the flow of their learning. Why we're learning to lead climb will affect how we learn, how we accede to influence, and the risks we are willing to take. Second, we'll take a close look at lead climbing movement. It's not the same as toproping. Trailing a rope while we lead creates hazards that we must manage and continual chores that we must have the stamina to perform correctly. We also have to learn to fall, which is a movement skill, believe it or not. Falling is a way of moving, and falling well takes practice. Third, we'll get into the technical aspects of leading: managing the rope, clipping the rope, clipping the anchors, and communication. Last but not least, we'll explore lead belaying.

Motivations and Lead Climbing Pathways

It's important to understand that there are lots of reasons that a first-timer might want to learn to lead. Maybe a climber's partner or peer group want(s) to learn, and there is a motivation to keep the partnership together. Maybe a climber wants to be able to use the entire climbing facility, including the lead climbing–only sectors. Some climbers are attracted to the added challenge, exhilaration, and risk of lead climbing. Some climbers see lead climbing as a vital skill to learn before making a transition to outdoor climbing. And some climbers don't care about leading at all, but they do want to be effective lead belayers. Let's examine how these motivations inform a lead climbing pathway that might be distinct and unique to each climber that pursues them.

If a climber simply wants to learn to lead in order to stay in a climbing partnership or among a peer group, then personal challenge and complex risk management are a low priority. It's important to focus on sound movement, technical ability, and belay abilities. We characterize this as the Infrequent Falls pathway. This lead climber will self-select climbs that are well within her climbing abilities, where falls are unlikely. She will learn how to fall, but she will probably be unlikely to take many falls. She'll learn to be technically adept at managing the rope, clipping, and using anchors, but she'll perform these tasks out of quotidian necessity. Mostly, she'll focus on being a good belayer, and giving her peers and partners great support and a great catch. Her leads enable her partners to rest, which is more important

Not all lead climbs have to be severe, strenuous, and intimidating. Some lead climbs can actually feel casual and rhythmic.

than any great personal satisfactions she feels from lead climbing.

A completely separate pathway is the Falls Frequently lead climber. Whether he is learning to push himself in lead climbing in order to transition to outdoor climbing, or simply for the joy and satisfaction of challenging himself in the gym, the Falls Frequently leader self-selects climbs that he can barely climb, or that he falls from routinely. This lead climber learns to fall frequently because it is impossible to explore and push the boundaries of one's abilities without climbing at the very limit of one's abilities.

Lead climbing pathway	Motivations	Climb choices and preferences
Infrequent Falls	Leads because partners lead.	Climbs are well within climbing ability and adjacent to their fellow climbers.
	Leads simply to explore the entire gym.	Develops enough lead climbing ability to climb the least difficult lines in lead sectors.
Falls Frequently	Leads for personal challenge and exhilaration.	Selects climbs that are both barely possible and impossible to push personal limits.
	Leads to prepare for outdoor climbing.	Selects climbs that demand more complex risk management, with a likely fall probability.

Motivation Questionnaire

When you go toproping or bouldering, how often do you find yourself going for a move, unsure of the outcome of your attempt, and taking a fall if you don't make it?

> 1. Never.
> 2. Occasionally.
> 3. Every time, unless I make it.

When you go toproping or bouldering, do you cycle through a warm-up set, followed by difficult problems that you can typically complete, followed by new projects?

> 1. Never.
> 2. Occasionally.
> 3. Every session.

Do you initiate climbing gym outings or do your climbing partners?

> 1. My partners always initiate.
> 2. Sometimes I initiate.
> 3. I always initiate, or I go alone.

Do your climbing partners also climb outside? Have they invited you to join?

> 1. Only inside.
> 2. Inside for now, but we're all interested in outside.
> 3. Inside and outside.

Add up your scores.

If you scored between 4 and 6, you might be in the Infrequent Falls pathway. Keep this in mind as you learn to lead climb. You want to learn how to lead and belay safely, you want to know what to do if you ever do fall, but falling might not be a regular part of your lead climbing.

If you scored between 7 and 9, you might not know your exact pathway until you start to learn to lead climb. You might discover that falling creates anxiety and you might not want to lose control. In that case, the Infrequent Falls pathway is a good place for you. You might discover a kind of exhilaration that you enjoy, and you might start down a Falls Frequently pathway.

If you scored between 10 and 12, remember that all your eagerness will be quickly halted if you don't learn some fundamentals and develop a relationship with a good belayer. Also, don't forget that becoming a good belayer makes it easier to meet a good belayer. Attention to details will enable your Falls Frequently pathway.

Movement

Regardless of your motivations for leading, there is a lot to learn to enjoy lead climbing safely. One of the first things you can do is practice your movement. It's easy and convenient to practice movement while trailing a rope by simply tying in to both ends of your toprope.

At first, it will feel unfamiliar to have a rope dangling behind you while you climb, but soon you'll

Tying in to both ends of the rope allows a climber to practice clipping and lead climbing movement with the security of a toprope. Just don't forget to unclip on the way down.

start to become familiar with the sensation. Eventually, you will even develop an awareness of the rope position. You will be able to feel it brush against your calf or your ankle, and those sensations will instantly inform you of the position of the rope, without even looking.

It's vital that you learn to move around the rope, appreciating that the rope can create a tripping hazard if it drifts behind any part of your body before a sudden fall.

In general, the connection of the rope line relative to the path of the climbing creates an opportunity to inadvertently create a tripping hazard. If the climber takes a wide athletic stance and the rope is clipped directly underneath the climber's position, the rope line will bisect the angle between the climber's legs. If the climber were to fall, tripping on the rope would be unlikely.

Tripping is a hazard while lead climbing. When the rope drifts behind the climber's leg, a sudden fall can upend or "trip" the climber.

Try to step around the trailing lead rope so sudden falls don't capture limbs behind the rope.

However, if the climber were to make a single move laterally, the tripping potential emerges. If the climber moves to the left of the rope line, there is a potential for the rope to drift behind the right leg.

Instead, the climber steps around the rope, bringing the rope line to the far right side of his/her legs and body.

Each connection point between the rope and the climbing surface creates a new rope line and a new fall line.

The fall line is the direction the climber will fall at any given time. It is the line directly beneath a climber's center of gravity. The rope line is the path the rope

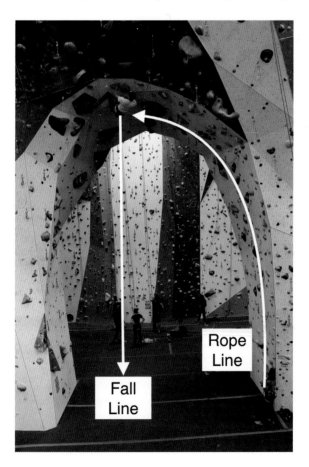

Rope Line

Fall Line

travels through all the quickdraws. A leader will want to select clips that keep the rope line straight or traveling through a gentle arc.

Once you've mastered the sensation of trailing a rope and the subtle dance of climbing around the rope line and the fall line, it's time to practice prioritizing stance. Deploying the same rope trailing exercise, climb up to the quickdraws on the wall. Don't bother trying to clip to rope into the quickdraws; that will come later. Instead, climb up and position yourself relative to a quickdraw; the quickdraw should be somewhere between your upper thigh and armpit. It might be directly in front of you, or to your right or left. Once you've positioned yourself in this clipping zone, relative to the quickdraw, reach out toward the quickdraw with whichever hand is most practical and snap your finger three times.

In this exercise, you're going to learn a lot about how the chore of clipping takes stamina, and prioritizing the position of your body, your footing, and the hold that you maintain while clipping will help you realize that a good stance is vital to making a good clip. While you're up there snapping your fingers, ask yourself some important questions:

Am I barely able to hang on long enough to snap my fingers?

Do I teeter off my stance every time I let go with one hand?

Does the snapping chore make me so tired that I can't even make it to the top?

These are all good clues that you'll need to keep practicing. You'll eventually develop enough stamina to charge through poorly selected stances, or you'll learn to prioritize the stance when clipping. We'd recommend the latter; it'll serve you better in the long run.

Technical Skills, Managing the Rope Line, and Communication

Since you've taken such care to learn your movement skills, you'll want to devote some time to technical skills. There are a few to cover. You'll want to learn to clip the rope into the quickdraws, pay attention to the rope line, and clip the anchors.

When it comes to clipping the rope into quickdraws, we've seen hundreds of descriptions, illustrations, and photo sequences attempting to show how this fairly innocuous skill is executed. It's just not that complicated, and the boogeymen that are out there seem like nominal concerns to us. If you practice clipping, and learn to clip, and add that skill into a careful progression of skill acquisition leading up to your first lead climbs, you will likely have the muscle memory and the unconscious competence to avoid many of the vague nightmare scenarios that persist.

But you've got to put the time in; you've got to learn to clip before it really matters. It is actually an enormously variable set of hand motions and body positions that you are trying to master, so don't get impatient. If you analyze all the variables, you'll see how many movements you need to master.

With so many variations in body position, handedness, and direction of gate opening, and with all the variables among those categories, there are hundreds of subtle differences for each and every clip. It will take time to experience each of them once. It will take even more time to become familiar and adept at

Clipping Variations	Compounding Variables		
Vertical body position relative to quickdraw	3-inch increments between upper thigh and armpit		
Direction of gate opening relative to clipping hand	Gate facing away from clipping hand	Gate facing toward clipping hand	
Clipping hand	Right hand	Left hand	
Clipping hand relative to body position	Reaching across the body	Reaching in front of the body	Reaching beside the body

each of those variations. There are dozens of recommended techniques, but don't spend too much time looking at books and illustrations. Pushing a rope into a carabiner, snapping it in, clamping it in, thumb flipping, Vulcan neck pinching: It's all just putting a rope into a carabiner. You'll get there soon enough. Be patient and have fun with it.

A great exercise to practice clipping involves a clipping classroom. These learning environments exist in some gyms, but they can be improvised in almost any facility. A clipping classroom lets you practice movement, clipping, and the hundreds of variations without getting very high off the ground.

Every clip will need to consciously manage the danger of backclipping. Backclipping is another of the much-maligned boogeymen in lead climbing. It's a real hazard, no doubt, but it's difficult to actually make it happen. It can be avoided altogether if the hazard is understood and managed.

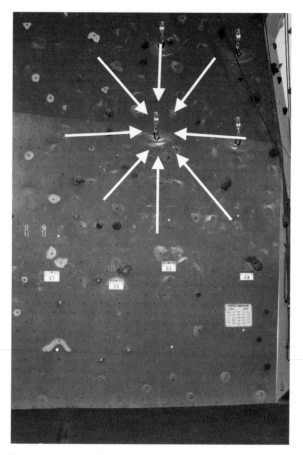

At almost every climbing wall, there is a place to practice clipping. Be sure to practice all the variations. Circumnavigate a quickdraw, practice with both hands, and practice every minute clipping sequence.

When the path of the rope line does not travel through a carabiner correctly, falling climbers can accidentally unclip their rope from the carabiner that is supposed to catch them. Falls become unnecessarily long, and the risk of ground fall increases. If we imagine that an imaginary plane runs infinitely in all directions, expanding away from every quickdraw, we would notice two things. First, we'd notice that the quickdraw plane is usually parallel to the wall plane. Second, we'd notice that our own bodies occupy a space in front of the quickdraw plane, while the climbing wall resides behind the quickdraw plane. To avoid backclipping, it's important that the rope line always travels on the wall-side of the quickdraw plane, while the climber's tie-in and the climber him/herself travels on the climber-side of the quickdraw plane.

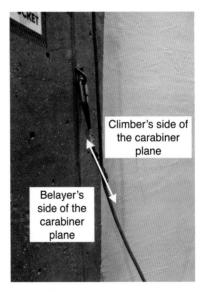

A lead climber must perceive that the carabiner's position creates a plane that is parallel to the climbing surface. That plane divides the belayer's side of the carabiner from the leader's side of the carabiner.

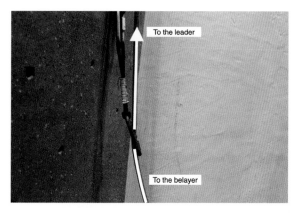

To clip correctly, the rope always travels from the belayer along the climbing surface and leaves the carabiner's plane toward the leader's side of the plane.

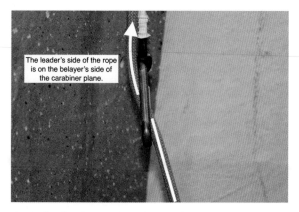

Backclipping is easy to recognize because the leader is climbing on the belayer's side of the carabiner plane. In this configuration, the rope can easily unclip the carabiner's gate in the event of a leader fall.

This concept, and the instinct it engenders, is important to any lead climber. It's easiest to practice on low-angled and vertical climbs, and it's on those climbs that the technique should be mastered. On overhanging features, the guiding principles of quickdraw planes are impossible to discern. Instead, a climber relies on a fundamental understanding of the backclipping hazard, and an instinct for how a climber's body position relative to the rope line and the fall line dictates the ideal way to put the rope inside a carabiner.

Clipping is an important skill, but it's also important to realize that a leader can't just clip any quickdraw he/she chooses. The selected line of quickdraws has to correspond to the line of the climb. In general, a lead climber wants the path of the rope's travel to be as straight as possible. At the very least, when the rope

Select quickdraws along the climb such that the rope line remains straight or follows a gentle arc.

changes direction, the direction should be consistent and gradual. An arcing rope line is not straight, but it is sometimes unavoidable.

By contrast, a rope line that alternates direction changes or makes acute direction changes will create so much rope drag that a leader will be completely unable to move at a certain point.

Finally, clipping the anchors is the last skill to perform to complete a lead climb. Some facilities are very much aware of how desperately an exhausted climber wishes to get the rope into the anchor, so the anchors are situated for quick *click-click*, take, and lower.

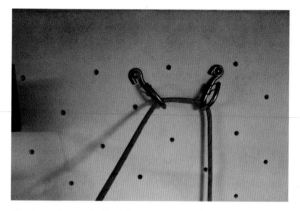

Anchors for lead climbing come in a few varieties. These quick clip shuts are fast and convenient.

Other anchors require the leader to have enough stamina to get a pair of opposite and opposed carabiners clipped before the sweet relief of a lower. In this case, clipping the anchor requires the same kind of stance and one-handed stamina that any quickdraw

Opposite and opposed carabiners are also common lead climbing anchors. They take a little longer to clip.

would require, but the leader has to get the rope correctly into two carabiners instead of just one.

The same communication techniques that toproping will likely have instilled in a toprope climber will also be valuable to a leader. The need to double-check all critical links is the same, and the need for a climber

Clipping the rope into the anchor cleanly avoids twisting and awkward loads on the anchor.

and belayer to have an unambiguous understanding of what is happening when is the same. Lead belaying simply has some slightly different actions that a climber may need to communicate to a belayer.

Let's review the entire communication sequence. First, the climber will ask the belayer if he/she is ready to belay. "Are you ready to belay?" The climber and belayer will double-check all the critical links in the system: knots, harness buckles, rope stack and closed system, belay device setup, locked carabiner. At this point, the climbing team will want to double-check one more little detail that is less important when toproping: Are there other parties crossing my lead climbing path, and does my climb cross paths with a party that is already climbing?

When toproping, the dynamics of a falling climber are not severe enough to seriously injure other climbers, as long as their belays are effective. In lead climbing, however, dynamic body masses produce enough force to cause serious injury if they were to collide. So double-checking to make sure the climbing path is clear should be part of the double-checks.

With the system double-checked and the belayer's readiness clearly communicated, the lead will begin leading. Along the course of that lead, the leader may need to rest on the rope. You will hear all kinds of words being used to communicate this simple action. We recommend "Tension!" as opposed to more colloquial options like "Take!" or "Take me tight!" "Tension" is a distinct two-syllable communication, and it's not easily confused with other commands.

Even though a belayer should be ready to catch a fall no matter what, it is also courteous and wise to announce a fall. Calling out "Falling" gives the belayer

There are no other climbers in the vicinity, above or on adjacent climbs. The climb is clear for the belayer to set up the rope.

a millisecond headstart on the catch he/she is about to perform.

We would also defer to the language and communication preferences of any climbing party on these two commands. It's not important what words the team decides to use. It is vital, however, that the words are prearranged, agreed upon, their meaning unambiguous, and their pronunciation concise.

Lead Belaying

Lead belaying is not easy. It's not something that you can learn to do well quickly. It takes practice. Eventually, good lead belayers learn how to do a few things really well. They learn to set up the rope in the right spot. They learn to give the perfect amount of slack, not too little, and not too much. They also learn a lot of techniques to help the lead climber when he/she needs it. For example, lead belayers know how to catch falls in just the right way, they learn how to help a leader rest on the rope, and they learn how to help a leader recover his/her high point after a fall.

Lead belaying is about more than just giving slack and not letting go.

Getting Set Up

When giving a lead belay, figure out where the fall line is for the first clip. Then stand directly beneath it, and then take one step off the fall line. This is where you will want to stand so the lead climber doesn't fall on your head. Once you decide where to stand, stack the rope up neatly on your brake hand side, in a nice neat pile, right next to your stance. Also, put a knot in the opposite end of the rope and position the knot so others can see it. Then hand the top end of the rope to your climber. He/she will tie in while you set up your belay device.

Communicate and double-check each other. As mentioned above, taking the time to establish an agreed-upon system of commands to communicate

Fall line

Take note of the slightly off fall line set up of the rope stack and the knotted rope end.

precise actions is important. It's also valuable to a climber and belayer to simply forecast the climb that is about to happen.

"You know what, I'm just trying to warm up on this one, but I'm feeling a little stiff. Will you just watch me closely when I'm moving and when I'm clipping. I shouldn't have any trouble with this climb, but who knows."

Or

"Jeez, this looks challenging. I think I'm going to either fall or take on every single quickdraw. Are you ready for this?"

Or

"I know I normally don't fall on climbs like this one, but I'm feeling super tired. Watch me at the top. I'm probably going to run out of energy."

Giving Slack

Appropriate delivery of slack is subtle. It's supposed to be just right. Not too little, not too much. You don't want the leader to even feel the slightest amount of resistance from your belay, nor do you want to provide a superfluous amount of slack, which could allow the leader to hit the ground. Many assisted braking devices offer the greatest economy of movement when delivering slack to the lead climber. Even though many belayers assert that ABDs have cumbersome mechanics that can result in a jammed rope and an inability to provide adequate slack, most of these assertions

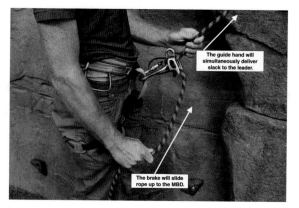

The guide hand will simultaneously deliver slack to the leader.

The brake will slide rope up to the MBD.

Brake hand ready to deliver slack.

Having delivered slack, the guide hand must slide back down the rope

Having delivered slack, the brake hand must slide back down the rope

Brake hand and guide hand deliver slack.

The belayer cannot deliver slack again until the brake and guide hands are repositioned.

Brake hand slides back down the brake strand in order to begin the cycle anew.

An ABD allows for the brake hand to remain stationary while delivering slack to a leader that is continuously moving.

Brake hand ready.

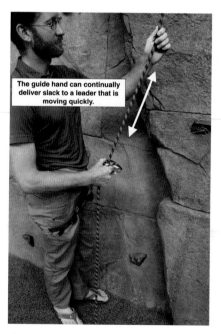

The guide hand can continually deliver slack to a leader that is moving quickly.

Guide hand feeds slack from the stationary brake hand.

are based on a lack of familiarity with the techniques needed to use an ABD to belay a lead climber.

The key to this movement economy involves a stationary brake hand. It might be helpful to see fundamental belaying with an MBD contrasted with an ABD to demonstrate this concept explicitly.

Many ABDs, by contrast, keep the brake hand stationary, eliminating an entire step in the belay cycle. As a result, there can be a 50 percent increase in overall efficiency when the belayer delivers slack to the leader.

This movement economy is especially useful on easy or moderate terrain, when the leader is unlikely to fall. One of the greatest hazards to the leader in that terrain might be getting tripped or snagged by an inadequate supply of slack from the belayer. In any case, it may be valuable for a belayer to opt for a belay tool and technique that provides slack to the leader as efficiently as possible while also adhering to the fundamental principles of belaying.

Compensating

Lead belaying also involves a subtle exchange of giving and taking rope called compensating. When a leader makes a long clip, there is a moment when the rope is actually clipped above the leader's head. So they're sort of on a 3-foot toprope. In this instance, the belayer will need to transition between giving slack, taking in slack, and seamlessly giving slack again.

The most extreme version of compensating happens when the lead downclimbs from a clip to a rest lower on the pitch, and then re-ascends to the high point. In that instance, especially, a belayer must alternate between giving slack and taking slack and seamlessly transitioning to giving slack again.

Providing Tension

Sometimes leaders just want to sit on the rope, and they don't want to slide down at all. They want to rest. When the climber calls "tension" the belayer knows

When the climber calls for a take, the belayer takes a mini hop, pulls slack through his/her belay system mid-jump, and then lets his/her counterweighted body pull all the stretch out of the climbing rope.

he's not going to make it any farther and just needs to sit on the rope. When the belayer hears those words, she's got to pull all the slack out of the rope. But there is still some stretch left in the rope. She'll want to pull that out too. So she reaches up high, and then quickly pulls down while hopping up, and yanking slack through her belay device. At that point, her full body weight is actually hanging on the rope and that pulls all the stretch out of the system.

Catching Falls

The most important part of catching a fall is stopping a leader from hitting the ground, or a ledge, or protruding holds. The second most important thing is minimizing the size of the fall without causing the climber discomfort. That's actually trickier than it sounds, and it has led to a lot of confusion among belayers. Often the concern that a lead fall will be uncomfortable overshadows the reality that all lead falls are dangerous. Every year dozens of accidents happen because a belayer is too concerned with giving a "soft" catch, so concerned that he/she actually allows the climber to fall all the way to the ground.

The idea behind these misguided intentions is not unfounded. When a climber is climbing an overhang, having too little distance between the tie-in and the previous quickdraw connection results in an abrupt and jarring halt. We might think of this as a "hard" catch. By contrast, adding an inconspicuous and precise amount of slack to belay allows the leader to land on a cushion of rope stretch and air beneath his/her feet.

When a climber has a larger mass than the belayer, this cushion is almost unavoidable because a dynamic mass tends to yank the belayer off his/her feet. When

The primary job of a lead belayer catching falls is to mitigate fall consequences.

a climber is significantly lighter than a belayer, the cushion might require a small hop. It takes practice. In general, when a climber is maneuvering through an overhang, the belayer will want to "encourage" or "ride" the fall, and that subtle interplay of rope is all that is needed to "soften" a belayer's catch. By contrast, when the climb is vertical or less than vertical, all the holds create tripping hazards, or they have the potential to turn an ankle or break a bone. In these falls, the belayer should be less concerned with "soft" catches and should be focused on mitigating the consequences of the fall. The belayer should "resist" or "fight" the fall, burying his/her own body mass into the counterweight, perhaps even using a ground anchor.

Batmanning and Boinks

When climbers fall they will usually want to return to their high point to resume climbing, and that will either involve batmanning or boinking. Batmanning is when climbers use the back side of their own

Climbing back up the climbing rope allows a fallen climber to get back to his high point, rest, and then make another attempt to climb the section where he fell.

counterweighted climbing rope to re-ascend. From the belayer's point of view, the climber introduces fits of slack on the belayer's side of the rope, and the belayer will need to quickly capture that slack while also asserting her own body weight so the climber doesn't lose his progress.

Boinking is harder, and many climbers won't have the physical strength to execute a boink. When

To belay a boink, the belayer must be suspended, and ready to both drop a little bit, when the climber boinks, and then pull slack through the belay without lowering or dropping the climber who is suspended from the counterweighted side of the rope.

climbers fall from an overhang, they are often suspended in the air. They are often unable to reach the back side of their climbing rope; if they could they would just batman up to their high point as previously described. So, the belayer has to maneuver a half body length up the counterweighted side of the climbing rope such that his body is suspended 3 to 4 feet off the ground. The climber then reaches overhead, grabs the climbing rope as high as she can reach, and then pulls all of her weight up, introducing a small loop of slack between her gripped hands and her tie-in. As she quickly releases this loop, a portion of that slack drops the suspended belayer, while the other portion drops the suspended climber. In portioned and strenuous increments, the climber can re-ascend to her high point, or get to a point where she can reach the climbing rope in order to batman. Whew!

Falling

Falling is one of the hardest movement skills to master, and many instructors seem to think that an overt form of exposure therapy is the best way to learn. We don't think so. Imagine falling as the most counter-intuitive experience that you could ask your body to perform. Gymnasts, acrobats, and airborne extreme athletes might approach falling intuitively, but the rest of us have a lot of work to do. For most of us, the rate at which our bodies are moving when we fall is unfamiliar, the forces involved in impacts when masses are moving at high rates is also unfamiliar, and the aggravating factors of the rope, ledges, and tripping are definitely unfamiliar.

We learn to fall by teaching our minds that falling is not something that happens to us, like tripping. Falling is something that we actively do. A climber is not the passive recipient of a fall; a climber actively falls and preserves him/herself in the process. For most, that mental adjustment is huge. We also learn to fall by conditioning fall instincts that enable us to deal with irregularities while we fall. There are actions that we should learn to reflexively execute, every time we fall. If we do these things, we'll not only be falling well, but we'll be able to adapt our movement and our tactics to deal with problems along the way. Once we've trained our minds and our bodies to reflexively react to falling with conditioned behaviors and actions, we can start practicing falling.

When falling, it's important to develop a reflexive response to the fall by actively doing four things: looking down into the fall space, pushing breath out, bending the extremities, and responding to impact. It sounds like quite a to-do list, but with practice these actions become second nature. A new lead can use a simple progression to build up to actual practice on the wall.

Start with a simple curb or step, less than 6 inches high. Stand on the curb, facing away from the landing zone, and use your imagination to envision your position high up on the climbing wall. It's important to do the imagination part of the exercise. Some climbers even close their eyes. Slow your breathing and imagine the climb and an impending lead fall. Then, when you're ready, initiate the fall. Remember, you won't go very far; you're only 6 inches off the ground. Instantly, as soon as you initiate the fall, open your eyes, look down into the fall space, bend your elbows and wrists,

Falling:
-limbs bent
-eyes looking into fall
-exhaling
-ready to absorb impact

When falling, look down into the fall space, bend the limbs, forcibly exhale, and do your best to impact the wall smoothly and comfortably.

bend your knees, push breath out, and as you land absorb the energy of the impact by collapsing and rebounding.

Your success on the curb exercise will lead you to a slightly higher step. Try 12 inches. Try 2 feet. At each increment, you are trying to both ingrain your natural response to falling (looking, exhaling, bending limbs, absorbing impact) and get accustomed to the jarring sensation of impact. Almost all climbers' bodies are capable of sustaining these impacts if they are executed correctly.

Once you've practiced several dozen imagination sequences from 3-inch, 12-inch, and 2-foot steps, you'll want to move on to the next increment. At the next phase, you'll want to learn to apply those same fall responses to impacts on a vertical plane, and you'll need a toprope for that. Find a climb on a vertical face, and swing yourself off the fall line. You're trying to set up a pendulum swing, and a sideways impact. Once, you've swung yourself off the fall line, grab some holds, get some footing, and go back into that imaginary space. When you're ready, initiate the fall by pushing off the wall; you'll immediately start to swing back toward the fall line. Even though it's a sideways swing, you can still practice looking into the fall space, exhaling, bending the limbs, and absorbing the impact. This time, the impact on the vertical plane will require you to adjust your hand and feet to that new sensation. Many instructors have likened this fall position and sensation to catlike reflexes. That seems apt. The cat is not consciously doing anything though, and you probably are. You'll need to practice until your response is as unconscious as the cat's.

Once you've sustained those sideways impacts on a vertical plane, several dozen times, it's time for the next increment. You've ingrained your response, you've experienced impact in a vertical plane, now you need to adapt to downward direction of travel, not sideways.

For this exercise, climb up to the top third of a vertical climb. You don't want to be anywhere near the ground for this exercise. Grab some holds, get some footing, and then instruct your belayer to put

The belayer holds the slack in the guide hand but does not pull the slack through the belay device when the climber is practicing falls. The moment the climber falls, the belay releases this place-holding slack and prepares to arrest the fall with the belay device.

1 foot of slack into the toprope system. You know that you are only going to fall 1 foot, but get into the imagination space anyway. When you release from your holds and begin your 1-foot descent, practice all the fall responses: look down, exhale, bend the limbs, absorb impact. After your fall, climb back up, and try again. Keep going until you're ready for a bigger fall. Next, have your belayer give you 3 feet. Practice, practice. Try 6 feet. Practice the maximum fall distance you could potentially encounter in your gym. If your gym's quickdraws are 4 feet apart, you'll need to build up to practicing a 10-foot fall.

For this exercise, the belayer has a unique job. He'll need to have a firm brake hand on the rope, but there could potentially be 10 feet of slack piled up in front of that belay device during the most extreme version of this exercise. It's best to keep that slack in front of the belayer, not in front of the climber. The climber could trip on all that slack, so it's best to just pile that slack up in front of the belayer, get in the brake position, and await the climber's fall.

Once a climber has practiced all these increments of falling, the final phase of learning to fall involves real falls in a real dynamic counterweight scenario. If the incremental phases of the learning to fall progression felt natural and gradual, this last transition will feel pretty abrupt. No matter how much you practice, an actual lead fall creates impact forces that are difficult to duplicate in a toprope scenario. So go easy. Start with 1- and 2-foot falls, and do them on slightly overhanging climbs. You'll want a location that doesn't offer obtrusive impact obstacles, so don't start on a vertical climb for actual fall practice. Definitely avoid low-angled features. Also, remember that you'll have to climb back up to your point multiple times, so avoid overhangs that are so severe, you'll have to boink in order to batman back up the rope.

Eventually, you build up to practicing longer falls, and then you can practice on vertical terrain, then on lower-angled terrain. Throughout this process, your comfort and familiarity with falling will be sending you a clear and unequivocal message. Regardless of your motivations or your pathway for lead climbing, if the learning to fall progression presents barriers, fears, and anxieties that are insurmountable, or if you are not able to ingrain a consistent fall response to every single fall, lead climbing might not be the best way for you to enjoy the climbing gym. Falling is a real risk, and on any climb, it is also a real probability. If you can't learn to fall without injuring yourself, you'll be gambling on the outcome of every single lead climb. That doesn't sound like fun to us; it sounds scary and it sounds risky. Lead climbing is fun, but it's not worth the anxiety or the inevitable injury.

Seek Instruction and Guidance

Lead climbing is one of the most dynamic ways to enjoy your climbing gym. It's also one of the most dangerous. We'd love it if this book provided all the explanation you needed, but it's probably more realistic for you to imagine that this book is a good supplement to instruction and guidance from the instructors at your gym, a mentor, or a professional climbing instructor or guide. Learning to lead, learning to lead belay, and learning to fall are difficult to do in a few hours. It's more effective to devote time and energy, and maybe even some investment, into classes and instruction. When supplemented with professional instruction, the contents of this chapter will help get you on the sharp end as efficiently as possible.

Conclusion

The first-timer enjoys access to resources that are revolutionizing the perception of what climbing is and what it can be. It's an exciting time to get involved in a growing sport. And yet, much of what has always made climbing unique remains. A first-timer will not find a sustainable relationship with the sport if he/she does not manage to cherish the things that have endeared climbing to generations. A first-timer has to appreciate that personal challenge is an indivisible part of climbing. We have to appreciate that camaraderie and community binds every climber to the next. And we have to accept that managing risk is both enjoyable and obligatory.

If we cannot accept the nature of personal challenge, it will be nearly impossible to justify the arbitrary pursuit of climbing plastic holds, arranged in increasingly difficult sequences, on artificial walls. We enjoy being physically challenged, and we eagerly anticipate the small gains in expertise and fitness that permit us to get a little bit farther, to close out a coveted project, and overcome seemingly insurmountable obstacles. At the very least, we vicariously enjoy personal challenges as we support our peers, provide belays, and remind each other of the sweet rewards of persistence and dedication. To the uninitiated, climbing seems like the stupidest way to spend one's time. We'd argue that without an appetite for personal challenge, they are exactly right. The many failures we endure are extinguished by a brief and fleeting success, and that must naturally seem ludicrous to a non-climber.

If we are so reclusive that the congregated psyche of a busy climbing gym doesn't make us feel right at home, then a first-timer will quickly become a one-timer. Crowds might not be everyone's cup of tea, but the bonds of a climbing partnership are as solvent and dissoluble in the climbing gym as they are on great peaks. Community is community, whether it's a community of 200 or 2.

Lastly, the risks associated with climbing in the gym elicit a unique satisfaction when we both understand them and learn to manage them. That essential pursuit of adventure, even in the gym, can be found while toproping, while training, while bouldering, and while lead climbing. Similarly, even the simplest forms of climbing create moments of doubt, fear, and frustration. A first-timer learns to appreciate that being emotionally vulnerable invariably precedes emotional resilience. Similarly, technical skill, careful double-checks and communication, and proficiency enable us to responsibly endanger ourselves. When we emerge from that gambit time and time again, when we are both unscathed and strengthened by each outing, real risks result in real rewards.

At that point, whether a first-timer goes on to pursue outdoor climbing or not, you will be one of us. You can't be a first-timer forever, but you can be a climber for the rest of your life, no matter where or how you choose to indulge your passion.

About the Authors

219823189593*54*

Nate Fitch is a faculty member in the renowned Outdoor Education Department at the University of New Hampshire, specializing in climbing courses and programming. He lives with his wife and two kids in Durham, New Hampshire.

Ron Funderburke is an AMGA-certified rock guide. He is the AMGA SPI discipline coordinator, the education manager at the American Alpine Clubs, and a senior climbing specialist with the North Carolina Outward Bound School. Ron lives in Golden, Colorado, with his wife and sons.